SURFING
THE
TECHNO-
TSUNAMI

Catch The Wave, Transform Your Life

Paul Hornsey-Pennell

"You never change things by fighting the existing reality.

To change something, build a new model that makes the existing model obsolete."

R. Buckminster Fuller

Surfing The Techno-Tsunami

"Catch The Wave, Transform Your Life"

©2017 Paul Hornsey-Pennell

Published by Mellow Manuscripts Ltd
The Workshop, Lower Dean, Devon TQ11 0LS, UK

Reviews

"Every once in a while a book comes along that's a game-changer... and this book by Paul Hornsey-Pennell is one of them. The forward-thinking content will help you to alter your mindset in order to not only survive, but excel in the rapidly changing world we live in.

Having personally resigned from my full-time job in 2009 to pursue a career as an entrepreneur, I fully endorse what Paul teaches in the book."

Richard McMunn
The UK's Leading Book Publishing Coach
And Award-Winning, Bestselling Author

"I met Paul a while back now and I still remember the impact he had on me before I'd even heard about who he was and what he does. That's a testament in itself of the person that he is. He is, quite simply - genuine. As I've spent more time with him and looked at his work, Paul is someone who's making waves in his field, literally ☺

He's there to help people and has some core principles that you can follow directly or easily adapt to suit what's right for you.
Keep up the great work, brother."

Ed JC Smith
Multiple 7-Figure Business Owner

"Paul's book identifies that there is a turning tide in the way people want to work. The era of working until you retire and then attempting to enjoy the fruits of your labour is long gone. There's a huge shift away from the 'it's got to be hard graft' mentality, and with emerging tech, it's gathering momentum.

So what's next?
And where does that leave you?

If you're asking, then this book will serve as a guide to help you answer some of those questions. Paul explores Job 2.0 and invites you to come on that journey with him. He offers hope for the future - opportunity, excitement, financial rewards and a new version of the 'daily grind' that will serve you better.

This book is packed full of information that would take you forever to gather yourself - so get stuck in. It's jet fuel for your plans. You don't have to be the next Zuckerberg, or Musk, but perhaps you can be the next Interpreneur, create your own fortune, enjoy what you do, and help others to do the same.

Read it, take action and ride your wave!"

Simon Coulson
Multiple 7-Figure Business Owner

"This is the wake-up call that my industry has been waiting for. The insights in this book give the clearest sense of the extraordinary possibilities for those who choose to step into a new way of thinking.

Embrace this information - it's world changing, which is desperately needed."

Steve Mitchell
Top 20 Global Network Marketer

"We are living in one of the most exciting times in human history and we are at a pivotal point, where technology and entrepreneurship are seeing an unprecedented convergence – you have a phone in your pocket that you can launch a global business from!

In Paul's book, which is brilliantly written and perfectly timed, he shares many insights into this incredible era, and also tells how you can get your piece of the pie!

In this clever, insightful and encouraging book, Paul covers, evaluates and explains a wide range of opportunities, that we all have access to, and his writing style is reasoned, objective, down-to-earth and encouraging – so it's easy to follow and understand, even for the most technophobic – and he helps you see how you too, can make the most of these opportunities and thrive in today's modern world."

Paul Preston
The HMO Guy and £multi Million Property Owner

"An extremely comprehensive summary of the problems that many will inevitably face in the coming months and years. The fact is, if you're not adapting to the changing economy, you'll be left behind.

This book not only outlines the issues, but (refreshingly) also gives real tangible solutions for those who may be affected."

Nick James
Copywriting and Product Launch Expert

Contents

Dear Reader,

There can be little doubt that we are living in one of the most extraordinary periods in our history, heralding a time when not only is the way that we work being transformed and redefined but the very way that we live our lives.

As we have progressed through each "age" in history, it has been defined by the technology of the day bringing with it new advancements, enabling the next stage of progress to occur. In each transition, the old makes way for the new and with it comes a period of uncertainty, anxiety and even fear, as old familiarities disappear in the face of change.

This time, however, there is one significant difference. The change is no longer about technology enabling us to do our job more efficiently and reduce costs. In many cases, it is about technology replacing us altogether.

With the prospect of 120,000,000 job losses in the UK and USA alone, and 1 billion worldwide, "think tank" organisations are stating that "robots and smart machines will have a higher IQ than 99% of humans" by 2030. So, now you begin to comprehend why I used the term "tsunami".

And yet, the irony is that the very technology that many consider is about to bring with it such destruction, also brings the possibility of a truly unparalleled quality of life, liberating millions from the restrictions of the very jobs that will be lost!

I believe that the increasing and crippling levels of stress in many people's lives is no way to live and the dial is only going to get turned up.

I also believe that we deserve better and that it's time we stopped looking to politicians for an answer. The truth is that we have very little time, and the political thinking is too limited and often compromised by self-interest.

I wrote this book because people are being kept in the dark, (intentionally, I believe) and because "we the people" deserve better: pretending life is going on as normal is not going to do it any longer. In fact, one of the most damaging mindsets you can take is that we are going to "get back to normal." Normal has gone, this transition is about creating a new "normal" which is a part of the reason so many people are unsettled in themselves.

We first need to understand what is coming our way so that we know what we are dealing with and from there, we can look at the options that are available and make our own informed choices.

In parts, this book is a tough read, but once you get over the "hump", you will discover that the options available to all ages, backgrounds, sexes, races and religions are truly breathtaking in the possibility of personal liberation and creation of a culture where there are no restrictions other than those you set upon yourself.

Uniquely, this book is not just for entrepreneurs, as there is no shortage of books on that subject, but it is also for the 80% of people who don't identify with or want to be an entrepreneur and, given the scale of job losses, this 80% NEED to be addressed.

As you progress through the chapters, there are three things to remember:-

1) the possibilities in life are now unprecedented and unlimited;

2) you have to work at them and

3) we need to inform ourselves and each other NOW.

This book is the front of an awareness campaign, because the social and economic devastation that will occur if this tsunami were to hit us unprepared is incomprehensible. It is not inconceivable that there would be social unrest on a huge scale. Having said that, we can avert it, but WE must begin to recognise that it's down to us.

With that in mind, I ask that you like and share our Facebook page www.bit.ly/fbbookreview so that, together, we can get as many people as possible out *of the way of this oncoming tsunami and enable them to catch the wave and transform their lives.*

Finally, because there is so much "stuff" trying to grab your attention in each moment, I want to grab it with this one question because this could have the most profound effect on your life.

So the question is ... If I knew that there was a tsunami coming (a real one) and that it was heading straight for you and your family, what would you want me to do?

You see, the thing about a tsunami is that for the vast majority of its journey it is barely detectable ... the wave is barely visible at just one foot tall ... not much, right? But here's the thing ... a tsunami travels under water at 500 m.p.h. ... that's the same speed as a commercial jet ... and it's only as it approaches the coast line that it begins to increase in height.

So whilst your answer to the first question might be "I would want you to call me and tell me to get out now!"... if I had done, you would have looked out and possibly seen a 1 foot high wave. What would your response have been to that? Most likely not take it or me seriously ...

However, the signs are there ... the wave is moving fast and is becoming visible. Check out our

Facebook page and see for yourself at
<u>*www.facebook.com/surfingthetechnotsunami*</u>

Your answer needs to be "don't accept a NO from me, as my answer!"

Read the book until you totally get ... there's a tsunami coming.

Surf's Up.

Paul

Chapter 1

Take The Red Pill

"You can't call it that, it will frighten them. It's frightening me! People don't want to be frightened, they want to be encouraged."

I was in a meeting with a consultant who charges eye-watering fees to write key speeches for CEOs of multinationals and create presentations designed to win eight-figure contracts for their companies. Clearly she knew her stuff and I wanted her opinion on the title and theme of the book you are now reading. I had been discussing that, in my view, most people have no idea as to the degree of change that is fast approaching or the possibilities that are coming with it and that the title needed to grab their attention. However, this was not quite the response I was hoping for.

"If this was to appeal to me" she said, "I would want to be encouraged, not frightened. If I were a single mum, early forties, back from work, tired and fed up, I would need to be encouraged."

"But that's what is implied in the title of the book" I replied, somewhat defensively.

"I disagree. As soon as I read the word 'tsunami', I have an image of a physical tsunami in my mind. It's almost overwhelming" was her response.

The interesting thing was that we were both irritated. Her at what she was imagining and me because she wasn't telling me that this was completely brilliant! The other interesting thing was that this wasn't, by any means, the first time I'd had this response.

In the countless seminars and talks that I have given since the mid-'90s (pre-internet ... how did we manage??), I have heard the tension in people's voices and seen the look of concern, anxiety and even fear on people's faces as they try to contemplate something that we actually cannot comprehend. The only difference between then and now is that the expressions are more pronounced as the timescale gets shorter ... much shorter.

Clearly I chose to ignore her advice, but it has taken me four further rewrites to arrive back at the original title, precisely because it needs to get people's attention. Whilst there is no need to panic, there is certainly a need to wake up ... or perhaps, look up. My intention is that this book will make you aware of some of the information that most days I am forwarded regarding what is being discussed and implemented "in techno-land". By being informed, you are then able to make a clear choice and to take appropriate action and, I reiterate, whilst the levels of change are incredulous, so too are the options that are now available and the accompanying level of lifestyle for those who choose to step up into a whole new way of life.

In the movie "The Matrix" there is a scene where the two lead characters, Neo and Morpheus, meet for the first time. (If you haven't seen it I encourage you to do so - it's a fantastic concept.)

Neo is to be shown "the big reveal", which is that The Matrix in which people think they are living is a complete illusion and that reality is very different. But before he is shown it, he is given a choice of two pills: Take the blue pill and "everything goes back to how it was" or take the red pill and "you stay in Wonderland, and I show you how deep the rabbit hole goes."

So, at the risk of being totally over-dramatic (and then again, maybe not) this book is my version of "the red pill" because, in all seriousness, it is quite possible that your map of the world will never be quite the same once you have absorbed its contents.

One other thing ... there is no blue pill ... Oops.

With regards to the consultant's perspective, I totally got it. Whilst I appreciate what technology enables me to do, I struggle with learning how to use it because my perspective in life stretches back pre-internet (vinyl and cassette generation and proud of it!) so researching and writing this book from the "tsunami perspective" has caused my own levels of anxiety imagining the possible impacts on world populations. With that in mind, I asked her one final question.

"Tell me something ... if there was a tsunami coming, a physical one, would you want me to clearly bring it to your attention, (I don't mean running about screaming 'we're all gonna die', I mean being clear and intentional with my message) or would you want me to encourage you?"

"I would want you to bring it to my attention so I was in no doubt."

"Good! Because there is something you don't seem to understand."

"What's that?" she asked.

"There's a Tsunami coming."

"The only way to make sense out of change is to plunge into it, move with it, and join the dance."

Alan Watts

www.surfingthetechno-tsunami.com

Chapter 2

From Monks To Mars

The truth is, the signs are everywhere that things are changing at an ever-increasing pace. In over 25 years of coaching businesses of all sizes, I believe everyone knows that change is coming and that many are anxious, not wanting to look up and see what's approaching and what it means to them. This is understandable as it raises the very real question: "Is this threatening my security?"

Even going for my early morning walk, I met up with one of my neighbours who works in technological systemisations of factories and businesses around the world.

"It's not going to be too bad" he said. "There will still be jobs". His tone told me that he was trying to convince himself, not me, and confirmed what I am hearing every day; while there will be jobs, even new jobs, it looks like it's going to be insignificant compared to jobs that will be lost.

"I don't think you understand" was my response, "I see all this advancement as a good thing. A really good thing! You do realise that the solutions are already here, don't you?" I asked. "The problem isn't technology; the problem is that people are all looking at this from completely the wrong angle."

"How so?"

"If you continue to look at the job as being 9 to 5, five days a week then you're missing the point. It's time to wake up and realise that the "new job" is not in the same structure. You have to let go of trying to recreate the old model <u>then</u> you get to see that what many people are already embracing as the new way forward is fantastic."

"Interesting" said my walking companion.

"There is one other thing that people are realising" I said, warming to the theme.

"What's that?" he asked.

"That for <u>countless</u> numbers of people, their job stinks and has done for a long time. In addition, it's going to get much worse. Cut backs, increased competition for jobs and the very efficiencies you are talking about, along with massive technological advancements, are continually adding massive pressure for stagnant pay and longer hours.

One of my neighbours is in the Police Force and she used to be one of seventeen officers covering a 200-mile area. Now she is one of two. ONE OF TWO! That means she is out on patrol on her own, hoping that she is going to make the next five years to pension without getting beaten up. Five years of hoping you are not going to get beaten up is a terrible way to live.

Another friend of mine worked with a company from the age of 17 and spent over 30 years literally working every position on his way up to the top as General Manager. He transformed a loss-making business into a profitable one before it was bought out. He was working 100 hours a week and took one day off in 4 months *including weekends* in order to ensure that the company maintained its profit. A HUNDRED HOURS A WEEK!

Not surprisingly, he ended up having to take time off for stress and depression. The company's response? They sacked him and accused him of defrauding the company's sickness scheme, refused to even pay owed holiday time, making it his responsibility to sue them and prove them wrong and you know why? Because sometimes he would not answer the owner's email within 24 hours! Utter bastards!"

The conversation came to an end as we approached his house ... "Let me know when your book is out would you? It sounds interesting."

As I walked down the High Street, I called in at the Post Office and Elizabeth, the Post Mistress, asked me how the book was coming along. (I live in a village with a wonderful community.) As we talked about the theme of the book, the look on her face totally nailed why I have written it. As with almost everyone who begins to get a glimpse of what is approaching, there was concern and confusion as she tried to comprehend the sheer scale of what I was telling her.

"But if all these things are happening and all these jobs are going to disappear then what's going to happen? What are people going to do?"

"Firstly," I replied, "the possibilities and the opportunities this technology makes available for the 'ordinary' person are on a whole new level, *if* they are willing to embrace them, and secondly," I went on, "what you need to grasp is that it's not '*if* these things are happening' … by all accounts they *are* happening, right now and it's all accelerating. I truly believe that for the majority of people, the career is dead. It's over. Finished. This is the wake-up call to look around and make some decisions.

So the only way to think about this is that it's not *if* but <u>when</u>."

The Post Office is a minute's walk from my home, both of which are in the village of Ide (pronounced "eed"), which in turn is just a short walk from Exeter. Exeter is a perfectly proportioned city that boasts the most handsome of cathedrals founded in 1050, almost one thousand years ago.

My home is in a row of seven cottages that collectively are called "The College". To get to us you must walk over a footbridge that drapes itself over a small river that, in turn, meanders past our front doors. It really is as idyllic as it sounds. (Look up Ide on Wikipedia, there is a photograph.)

Around 600 years ago, the monks from the cathedral lived in these cottages and would "commute" through the fields to "the office". So to have this historical backdrop when discussing the fantastical technological changes and the visionary projects of Elon Musk (creator of Paypal, owner of Tesla cars and SpaceX), who is pursuing return flights to Mars within 10 years and a populated Martian City within the next 40 - 100 years, is surreal.

Similarly, my impassioned conversation with Elizabeth about the "new way" was in complete contrast to the simple honesty of our little post office/community store with its home-made shortbread and pots of delicious local honey.

Interestingly though, by the end of the conversation, she was left in no doubt that both she and her teenage children would benefit from reading this book.

I took that as affirmation that this information is for everyone and of all ages, certainly in Ide, at any rate.

As humans and technology become intertwined, we will be freed up from laborious tasks and will seek more engaging and satisfying challenges. In fact, I would go so far as to say that this period is not just about how we work and make a living, but that we are transitioning into a new civilisation.

To give you a little taster, the Wall Street Journal reported that Mr Musk has a company called Neuralink that aims to implant tiny electrodes in the brain "that may one day upload and download thoughts." He has talked about the evolution of the smart phone through a "merger of biological intelligence and digital intelligence", in other words a "brain-computer interface" that he calls the "neural lace". (Download Google maps onto the iris by tweaking the ear lobe?)

He is not alone in this field, with Mark Zuckerberg (Facebook founder) rumoured to be funding research into technology that means you type using your brain waves. Others are also sinking billions of dollars into similar technology. Be clear - this IS happening.

As I turned left out of the Post Office heading back home, I posed the question to myself: "If Elon Musk offered me the chance to go to Mars, would I take it?" And as I walked across the footbridge that those monks had walked over, hundreds of years ago and reflected on all the chats in the Post Office and listened to the babble of the river and the sparrows constantly squabbling in the bushes alongside it, it became clear that I would have to turn Mr Musk down. Sometimes, for all the progress, the simple pleasures are what make a home, home.

Ok, so first we need to see what we are dealing with. Then we will look at our options. Here we go.

"Buckle your seat belt, Dorothy because Kansas … is going bye-bye."

The character "Cypher"
from "The Matrix"

Chapter 3

Surf's Up!

The fact that I could add to this chapter on a daily basis as new developments are announced, demonstrates the speed of what is approaching. As an example, today I got a text from my son informing me that Dubai are trialling robo-cops right now.

However, the fact that by the time you read this, some of these events will already have been eclipsed, demonstrates its sheer speed, so I need to prepare you in advance by telling you that this is a long chapter.

How you read it is up to you and I tell you now there is a lot to cover because these changes are everywhere. If you end up skimming through the sections, then I have a request to make ... if you see an industry sector that affects someone you know, then let them know about it.

This book is an early warning system and the intention is to give as many people as possible a "heads up" as to what's going on.

Let's get stuck in:

AMAZON GO

Everyone knows Amazon online but how about Amazon retail stores as well? How come? Surely online is "where it's at"?

Amazon recognises that people will always want to be able to physically go shopping, but they want the online convenience included and so they are trialling their "Just Walk Out" system in their Amazon Go stores.

The "inconvenience" of a convenience store, in their mind, is that after you have picked up all your items you then have to go and stand at a checkout and pay, so, at an Amazon Go you swipe into the store (doubtless an app will soon do this for you) and as you enter, computers and sensors track the items as you take them off the shelf and place them in your bag.

As you leave the store, your Amazon account is immediately charged.

That's it.

This has already been successfully trialled in Amazon's bookstores, of which they are rumoured to be creating an initial 400 in the USA alone.

Staff required? 3.

With supermarkets constantly battling in a price war, it is not difficult to see this model being introduced as a solution to their most expensive cost ... the store worker.

(Source www.bbc.in/2vkLh70)

Bye bye store workers?

UBER

Uber is acknowledged as the fastest growing company in corporate history.

Here is a brief history of its meteoric rise.

Founded in USA in 2009 it was initially called UberCab and was a black cab service. 2010 saw it launch as Uber in San Francisco where you could request a cab by text (text! ha!) and then 2011 saw it expand into New York.

In under a year from its launch in "San Fran", Uber went international, starting in Paris in 2011. Two years after that, Uber moved into India and Africa, meaning that within 4 years Uber was valued at $3.8 billion. Interestingly, Google Ventures invested in the company (a sign of how both these giants are thinking ahead).

2014 witnessed the first "offshoot" UberRUSH (bicycle courier/delivery service) launched, but also another clear statement of intent when $1.2 billion was raised, giving an overall valuation of $17 billion = 400% increase on its valuation in 1 year.

Also in 2014 the core product evolved and UberPOOL launched, allowing you to split the cost of the ride with another passenger going on a similar route. Carpooling goes techno!

2015 was yet another year where expansion took place in many different directions. UberCARGO includes all house/office moving and delivery requirements (Hong Kong initially) but also UberEATS was launched for on-demand food delivery in minutes. Starting with 4 pilot cities it's now in 93 cities making this more than a snack attack. (Oh come on that was a good one!)

However, still in 2015, a clear statement of intent as Uber buys the Mapping company deCarta AND opens its research facility into building self-driving cars. This progressed further by teaming up with one of the giants in car manufacturing and signing a "memorandum of understanding" with Toyota to see how they could work together.

Still more landmarks in 2016 as Uber registered its 2 BILLIONTH cab ride and Uber and Chinese rival Didi merged in a $35 billion deal.

"It took five years to reach our billionth trip, six months to reach the next billion … and we'll hopefully reach our third even more quickly," (founder, Travis Kalanick).

At the time of writing this book, June 2017, Uber now operates in 662 cities around the world and is valued at nearly $70bn (£55bn).

Now at this stage you might be thinking that this is the perfect model, surely it can't be improved? Travis Kalanick is on record as having said "The reason Uber could be expensive is because you're not just paying for the car - you're paying for the other dude in the car".

So, the next stage is to reduce the expense, or "dude" ... and the estimates say there are between 1 - 1.5 million "dudes" driving under the Uber banner.

Now the reason for Uber having sunk a huge amount of money into the driverless car concept becomes clear. So, here's a question for you: how far away do you think that driverless cars are from becoming a reality? 5 years? 10 years?

Are you ready for this? They're already here.

Uber took delivery of their first fleet of driverless cars in August 2016 in Pittsburgh.

Bye bye 1 million+ drivers? Maybe not all ... for now.

www.bloom.bg/2tR8srD

TRUCKING

This is an industry where in the USA alone there are 3.5 million truck drivers and in the wider industry there are 9 million related jobs.

www.bit.ly/2uhqh4e

Another relevant statistic (for the USA) is that the average salary of a truck driver in the USA is reported to be $40,000. So, just as a cab driver is regarded as the expensive part of the fare, the truck driver's salary is regarded the same way.

What's interesting is that when I say to people "Ok, so driverless cars have arrived, how far off do you imagine driverless trucks to be?", the majority of people still go to the fallback position of "10 years, 5 years at the ABSOLUTE soonest ...... right?"

Er ... they're already here too.

"On 6th May 2015, the first self-driving truck hit the American road in the state of Nevada."

Check out www.bit.ly/2vkJzSS for footage of Daimler's incredible self-driving truck.

On 25th October 2016, Uber's self-driving truck made the first delivery of 50,000 cans of Budweiser on a 120-mile delivery route. The driver takes the truck out of the depot onto the highway, then hands over to the onboard computer, leaving him free to complete paperwork in the back of the cab, until needed to take the truck off the highway into the delivery depot at the destination.

People's initial concern is the safety aspect, thinking that delivering cargo is somehow more complicated than driving a car, but consider that once a commercial flight has taken off, 95% of the flight is handled by a computer, until it is time to make the final approach. The same with container ships being operated by a skeleton crew. The truth is that 98% of accidents are down to human error.

Check out www.bit.ly/2tTcOg5

The co-founder of this technology, Leo Ron, is clear about where this is going:

"You can imagine a future where those trucks are essentially a virtual train on a software rail, on the highway," he says. He sees a day when trucks do their thing on the interstate, then stop at designated depots where humans drive the last few miles into town. Drivers, in effect, become harbour pilots, bringing the ship to port.

This following statement not only applies to trucks … it applies to ALL machinery that can be and will be taken over by a robot:

"Robot trucks also don't need salaries - salaries that stand to go up because fewer and fewer people want to be truckers. A company can buy a fleet of self-driving trucks and never pay another human salary for driving. The only costs will be upkeep of the machinery. No more need for health insurance either. Self-driving trucks will also never need to stop to rest, for any reason. Routes will take less time to complete."

However in the shorter-term, "For the foreseeable future, the driver will remain an essential part of the system. But with Otto, (the driving software) they can do something other than deal with the stress of driving. Like practice yoga."

To give you an idea of the savings, the brewing company that was involved in this first trial delivery estimates that they could save $50 million a year in the USA if they could deploy driverless trucks, even with drivers riding along to supplement the technology.

www.bloom.bg/2sY7S8u

If you find the whole "self-drive" conversation still seems too far-fetched, then I know for a fact that the major car companies, right now, are involved in conversations that are set to transform the transportation industry out of all recognition. It's happening.

Bye bye 3.5 MILLION truck drivers?

"Hey, Doc, we better back up. We don't have enough road to get up to 88 (mph)."

"Roads? Where we're going, we don't need roads."

(Marty McFly and Dr "Doc" Emmett Brown from the movie "Back to the Future")

VERTICAL TAKE-OFF, FULLY RECHARGEABLE DRONE TAXI

So, how're you doing? It's around about now you may well be feeling a little "wobbly" as your world is being challenged. If that's the case, then just recognise it as a normal response … and then try this out for size!

Uber are working on "Uber Elevate", which is intended to free up traffic and shorten commutes, with a two-hour commute turning into a 15-minute flight.

In effect, Uber is promising flying cars. They plan to have a network of fully electric, fully rechargeable, vertical take-off and land vehicles.

FLYING CARS! This is comic book stuff that I read about as a kid!

So, come on then, how far off do you think that this is from becoming a reality? 15 years? 10? 5? We're talking flying cars folks ... it's got to be ten years, right?

How about NOW?!

Dubai Roads and Transportation Agency have announced that they intend to (literally) launch their electric, fully rechargeable drone service "taking off" in 2017. The aircraft carries a single person 30 miles at around 100 mph. In fact, the brother of a friend of mine has already been up in it, on one of the test flights. He described this "pod" that you get into, which has four rota blades on each corner. You tap in co-ordinates into a digital pad and off you go! (Oh to see the look on your face right now.)

www.bbc.in/2tTyeK4

BUSES

Now you're getting into this, it should come as no surprise to read that buses are going driverless.

Quite literally, as I write this, trials have begun in London with a "driverless shuttle bus" that is run by a computer. It is anticipated that paying passengers will start using this service in 2019 and it's worth noting that they are not testing this for the shuttle's efficiency …. they already know it works; this is to begin to get the public comfortable with the idea of being in a vehicle with no driver.

Savings? There are currently around 25,000 bus drivers on an average salary of £24,000. That's £600 million in the UK alone. Imagine what that translates to in the USA.

Bye bye bus drivers?

www.bbc.in/2taWzOE

CONSTRUCTION

Rather than build a building, how about you print one out instead?

The idea of being able to physically print out a 3D building has been around for a while and has been encumbered by the limitations of the actual printer itself, but advances are being made that are resulting in buildings being printed out in considerably less time and, of course, at vastly reduced costs.

The world's first functional 3D printed office building opened in Dubai on 24th May 2016, having been constructed (or rather, printed) in 17 days. Construction time was reduced by 70%, labour cost down by 80%. No material waste (they calculate the amount of material needed and use it precisely).

www.bit.ly/2uqwtXS

China is a huge investor in this industry where they are printing 2-bedroom houses for around $5,000. Whilst basic in design, there is no doubt that as the printing technology is refined, so will be the houses.

With further reports of 3-storey properties being printed at a floor a day AND one Chinese company reported to be opening offices in 26 countries, with the Egyptian government reported to have ordered 20,000 houses, it could be that we are witnessing a radical change in the construction industry.

Imagine a proposed development of 3,000 houses and instead of construction trucks turning up with all the hustle and bustle that a small army of builders brings, there is a field full of printers, each one quietly printing out a house a day and then being moved to the next position for the next property.

Add to this the fact that you can already buy pre-plumbed, pre-wired house kits, then it is only a matter of time before you click on your Ikea app, pick out your drapes, furnishings, duvet covers (oh and remember those little t-light holders!) then click on the model house you want and a week later it arrives on the back of a truck, already decorated, with an "assembler" (not builder) who has a wrench to just bolt the two halves together after having crushed your existing property and hauled it away!

Bye bye house builders?

www.bit.ly/2tmIV5V

So, dear reader ... how are you doing? At around this time in my seminars, there is a look of overwhelm on some of the participants' faces as they try and make sense of it all. But given that we are in a time where factory workers in China are building robots that will ultimately take those human jobs, trying to make sense at this stage is almost pointless. My advice is to keep going with it and we'll get some perspective at the end.

FAST FOOD

ROBO BARISTAS... In February 2017, Cafe X opened its first robotic coffee shop in San Francisco (with the strap line "Don't settle for long lines and bad coffee.")

TAKEAWAY MEALS ... feeling hungry? Tap your "JustEat" app, place your order, go to pay and then ... hold on ... what?! "Is a delivery robot acceptable?!" ... er, sure! You receive a text, "Your meal has arrived." You open the door and see a kinda cute 6-wheeled relative of R2D2, with a flashing flag. Your meal has arrived. This is happening, now.

BANKING

The Bank of America is now (Feb/March 2017) opening branches with no workers at all. You go into the branch, sort your money out via an ATM (ha! and get a burger while you are there) and speak to "someone" via webcam, in the event you need to have a human interaction. This is not new by the way. In some countries, fully automated banks have been a way of life for over a decade.

Bye bye banking staff?

LAWYERS

IBM have a programme called Ross and are currently using it to research cases and to perform due diligence and are finding that efficiency gains are striking. Luis Salazar, a partner in a Law firm in Miami, tested it against himself by looking for two cases that were very similar. He spent 10 hours searching for information relevant to one case. "Ross" found the information for the other case, <u>immediately</u>.

When typing a legal question into "Ross", it replies with a few paragraphs summarising the answer and gives a two-page explanatory memo. The results "are indistinguishable from a memo written by a lawyer" Mr Salazar said. "That blew me away," he went on. "It's kind of scary. If it gets better, a lot of people could lose their jobs."

The advice given out by lawyers is measured at around 67% accuracy. The measured level of accuracy from the Ross? 92%.

www.nyti.ms/2tQB1p3

Cost? Software development and ongoing updates.

Cost of a lawyer?! Case dismissed!

Bye bye lawyers?

HEALTH CARE

The health industry is about to take a leap in this technological evolution.

SURGICAL ROBOTS

Surgeons have already performed tens of thousands of robot-assisted surgeries around the world. The surgeon uses a virtual system from their computer that links up with a robot in an operating theatre 400 km away. Having the ability to control 5 or 6 arms, the surgeon has more options than with a team of humans and with no human shake or error.

Hutan Ashrafian, a bariatric surgeon (specialising in obesity) and a lecturer at Imperial College, London, says it's entirely possible that medicine will eventually employ next-level surgical robots that have enough decision-making power to be considered artificially intelligent. Not only could such machines handle routine tasks, they could take over entire operations.

The results that are already being shown in industrial labs are demonstrating that the robots are more precise and efficient. If increased automation improves outcomes, there is no stopping it.

When you consider the salaries a surgeon commands, the cost savings and efficiency gains are incredible.

Bye bye surgeons?

www.bit.ly/2vkrXqj

COMPUTER DIAGNOSTICS

An area of massive efficiency is that of diagnostic testing. There are now programmes that can detect forms of cancer and run 50 different instant blood tests FROM YOUR SMART PHONE.

With political arguments over healthcare and healthcare costs, this will result in huge savings and as an early detection process could stave off disease in its early stages and avoid the prohibitive cost of treatment in a later stage.

If this isn't remarkable enough, when trialled in Rwanda for the testing of HIV, syphilis and other STD's, it took just 30 minutes of training for the basic care workers to be able to use one such programme run through a smart phone.

With almost instant results and no need to keep blood samples that previously needed to be taken to laboratories, you can see how this doesn't just reduce the requirement for doctors to provide a diagnosis, but how it also affects a wider range of jobs, such as laboratory work and support staff. It saves a huge amount of money as well as meaning that people who have basic medical training can now fill in a vital part of the support structure at a fraction of the cost, with a huge reduction in people required overall.

www.bit.ly/2vksc4H

It is easy to see how the trip to the doctor will, in the near future, only be necessary in the most particular of circumstances. This has the potential of saving £/$ billions and reducing the numbers of staff considerably.

Bye bye doctors?

As I sit here typing this, I am looking at a screenshot of a BBC article talking about "smart bandages" that are being trialled soon. The article starts "Bandages which can detect how a wound is healing and send messages back to doctors could be trialled within the next 12 months. The bandages would use real-time 5G technology to monitor what treatment is needed and also keep track of a patient's activity levels" say scientists.

"Wow this is incredible" is my instant response, swiftly followed by "Wait ... did they say 5G?!"

Bye bye nurses? (The answer is no but there will certainly be a radical shake up in what their duties are, which can only be a good thing.)

www.bbc.in/2uqWMgM

JOURNALISTS

With the phrase "fake news" very much in the ascendency at the moment, it may surprise you to know that currently around 10% of certain news/information services (e.g. Wikipedia) are produced by a robot. It is anticipated that in just 15 years, around 90% of ALL news will be produced by robots.

Bye bye journalists?

CAR MANUFACTURING

The car industry is in for the most tumultuous of rides, to the point where there is increasingly a view that soon, instead of owning a car, we will hire one, ordering it on a "car app". And already this isn't as far-fetched as it seems.

In hundreds of cities around the world, you can already use an app from a company called Zipcar and to quote directly from their website ... "Zipcar is far simpler and more convenient than conventional car hire. Once a member, when you need a car, just choose your make and model from the great selection parked around your local area; get in and drive off." You can hire it for an hour, a day, or as long as you wish.

Stanford economist, Professor Tony Seba, in a futuristic report, maintains that with the growth of electric cars, there will be no more petrol or diesel cars, buses, or trucks sold anywhere in the world within eight years. (I find myself struggling with this but what do I know?) The entire market for land transport will switch to electrification, leading to a collapse of oil prices and the demise of the petroleum industry as we have known it for a century. Dealers will disappear by 2024.

As the battery life in electric cars increases, he argues that it is a threat to Ford, General Motors and the German and Japanese car industry. They will face a choice between manufacturing electric vehicles in a low-profit market and reinventing themselves as self-drive service companies.

He goes on to state that these gigantic industrial model companies are now in the wrong business, being out-thought and out-developed by Google, Apple and Foxconn, who are going for the jugular. If you wondered where Apple might go next as it continues its evolution from being "just a computer company" then here's one part of the answer. Silicon Valley is looking to dominate the car manufacturing industry.

This not only means a total upheaval in the car industry, but also the supporting industry as well.

As one example, there are around 2,000 moving parts on a standard petrol/diesel vehicle, the majority of which are made in supporting businesses.

On a Tesla there are 18.

Tesla gives an infinite mile, infinite car-owner warranty, so the few parts that are on these cars are clearly meant to last. They will therefore need replacing much less often and, as a result, fewer parts require manufacturing.

When you then discover that Warren Buffet, probably the most successful investor in the world, has invested into the biggest Chinese electric car, it would seem the writing is on the wall.

Bye bye to the employees in the American, European, Japanese car companies and supporting industries?

Now do you see why I call it a tsunami?

ACCOUNTANTS / AUDITORS AND BOOK KEEPERS

One area that is expected to be among the hardest hit is that of accountancy. If you think about it, it makes perfect sense. Number entry and formulation is the basis of accountancy … it's what computers and software were made for.

Bye bye accountants AND book keepers?

ARMED FORCES

Warfare itself is beginning to even look like a computer game. Technology means that the use of people on the ground is needed less and that remote fire power offers a more "efficient" way of dealing with a situation. (I am not comfortable writing this but it is how it seems.)

With a salvo of cruise missiles launched from a ship or a submarine that can be programmed to go through the very window of the very building that is the target, or the use of a drone that is remotely flown, warfare can be operated with technology alone and none of the attacking forces' troops at risk. From the politicians' perspective, not having forces on the ground makes it more "palatable" and less likely to lose votes.

EDUCATION

It is already the case that over 50% of many degree courses are fully online and this will only increase. Schooling in general on the internet is going to increase massively and my own belief is that the entire structure of schooling will change beyond all recognition, as independent learning takes hold. The benefits are huge, offering a real diversity in subject matter and also link-ups with students from all over the world, engaged in real-time projects.

I also think that, because there will be a massive increase in the numbers of people working from home, increasing numbers of families will opt to have their children around them more, as socially we change our habits. The possibility of being able to offer a far more family-friendly way of life can only be a good thing for a society that so often feels more and more isolated, with the family unit under constant pressure.

I have a feeling that "the youth" will claim their place in our society, as they begin to recognise that their own uninhibited talent and imagination are perfectly aligned to work alongside this new technology and with that, their clear, uncluttered and uncompromised way of seeing the world will be able to be expressed.

FARMING

Farming has possibly seen the most visible benefits from technology and with it, the clearest impact on jobs. A century or so ago, it would take a whole team of people a few days to harvest a crop from one field. Nowadays, in the wheat fields of the USA, not only do they have fields that are singularly bigger than an old entire farm, but the tractors that cover them are completely unmanned. These are, literally, robots that genuinely look like they came out of RoboCop. As they "work the fields", they are linked up to satellite systems that give them complete feedback of the land gradient, and the consistency in planting, seeding and fertilising of the ground. Truly, this is an impressive piece of technology.

Animal care is also increasingly mechanised and whilst this raises moral issues for some, there is little doubt that this is going to progress as the entire process is increasingly systemised. With the use of additional technology introducing vertical tower systems, vegetables are now grown on a massively efficient scale.

Technology continues to be the driving force behind the planet's ever-increasing demand for food.

When you consider that farming in developing countries employs 48.2% of the population and in developed countries it's 4.2%, then you get a real comparison of the impact technology has had on jobs.

POLICE

Dubai is leading the way in many areas of technology, most likely because their city, being so modern, allows that more easily. A part of their cyber strategy is the introduction of police robots that are out patrolling the streets already. Currently, they can recognise faces and the public can use them to report crime, pay fines and get directions. They are not armed or programmed to say "Dead or alive, you are coming with me." (Robocop fans will get that one), however, depending upon how vivid your imagination is (or how much you want to scare the crap out of yourself), this too is not beyond the realms of possibility.

Bye bye police officers? No. However, it is reported that "multi-lingual, crime-fighting robots will make up a quarter of the city's police force by 2030, according to officials," so the co-operation between man and machine in this area is only just beginning.

www.dailym.ai/2taR2Yd

OTHERS

Other areas where an impact is anticipated exist right across the board and I could produce chart after chart from ever-increasing recognised experts, panels, commissions etc. Here are a few more for you to add to the list.

Check out these figures indicating the % likelihood of total computerisation:

TELEMARKETERS	99%
RETAIL SALES	92%
TECHNICAL WRITERS	89%
REAL ESTATE AGENTS	86%
WORD PROCESSING P/A	81%
MACHINISTS	65%
COMMERCIAL PILOTS	55%

(Figures from www.econ.st/2tTd0ME)

So what do you think? If you're feeling overwhelmed, then you are not the first to respond in that way and the reason for it is that this is an extensive list, covering huge areas of our day-to-day world. Literally, in the process of reading through this information, you are re-creating in your mind how your world is potentially going to be impacted.

As some of the articles/reports are directly from people involved in the tech world, it could be argued that they have a vested interest in getting this information out there, so I wanted to find out who is talking about it for purely economic (i.e. job) reasons.

<u>This</u> is where it begins to heat up ... considerably.

*"You can't stop the waves
but you can learn to surf."*

John Kabat-Zinn

www.surfingthetechno-tsunami.com

Chapter 4

Says Who?

When I read who was making statements about the oncoming transition, it got my attention. These people are not, for the most part, expressing a self-interest. Indeed, those who are involved in the tech world are actually expressing more concern than those not in it, because they see the future so clearly.

It was when I realised the sheer scale of their statements that the image of the tsunami came into my mind and you will see for yourself how appropriate it is.

What they state begs the obvious question, "Why are they not talking about this with a sense of urgency?" and when I look at what they are saying, the answer is clear ... they don't have a solution.

When I hear of a politician talking about "getting the jobs back", my response is that it's just (yet more) political speak aimed at calming people's nerves.

Either way, it's ok, because the answers are already here and if you choose to, you can take control of your own solution right now. My advice is: "Be proactive, catch the wave, you don't have time to wait."

So ... Who's saying what?

OXFORD UNIVERSITY & DELOITTE

In their collaborative "State of the State" report, Oxford University and Deloitte (a $37 billion global audit, consulting and tax advisory company) concluded that in the UK, there is a 77% probability of 1.3 million "repetitive and predictable" administrative and operative public sector roles being automated and that in the public sector alone, 850,000 jobs will disappear due to technology, robotics and the internet.

Deloitte's previous work has shown that all sectors will be affected by automation, with 74% of jobs in transportation and storage, 59% in wholesale and retail trades and 56% in manufacturing having a high chance of being automated.

Interestingly, in an additional report, Deloitte makes the case that over the last 140 years, automation has created more work than it destroyed. They are in fact the only group that predicts any kind of increase in jobs, but there are a number of factors that point against this happening:

a) There has never been automation on such a scale and with such potential.

b) Whilst these figures are for the UK, there has never been the capacity to implement global shifts on such a scale.

c) The speed of change is compounding (i.e. speeding up) because the advancements themselves go on to make faster advancements which go on to do the same.

www.blt.ly/2tTtYKl

I.P.P.R.

The Institute for Public Policy Research is regarded as the UK's leading, progressive think tank and in a landmark report entitled "Future Proof: Britain in the 2020s", they comment on how technological change will lead to greater emphasis on problem-solving, creative work and interpersonal skills over routine and manual tasks. "Different jobs will lead to ever more different lives."

They also state that within <u>15 years</u>, "*robots and smart machines will have a higher IQ than 99% of humans*" and then go on to say that "<u>it is a startling thought that 15 million jobs may be automated out of existence</u>."

STANFORD UNIVERSITY, Professor Tony Seba - Economist

In his report, "Rethinking Transportation 2020-2030", Tony Seba explains a number of scenarios that he is convinced will happen. (So, to be clear, that's less than three years from the point of writing this book.)

While I might challenge the timing of Professor Seba's claims, his broad point, that *"multiple technological trends are combining in a perfect storm",* looks beyond dispute.

"We are on the cusp of one of the fastest, deepest, most consequential disruptions of transportation in history," Professor Seba states. "People will stop driving altogether. They will switch en masse to self-drive electric vehicles (EVs) that are ten times cheaper to run than fossil-based cars, with a near-zero marginal cost of fuel and an expected lifespan of 1 million miles.

Only nostalgics will cling to the old habit of car ownership. The rest will adapt to vehicles on demand. Cities will ban human drivers once the data confirms how dangerous they can be behind a wheel."

"The 'tipping point' will arrive over the next two to three years as EV (electric vehicle) battery ranges surpass 200 miles and electric car prices in the US drop to below $30,000."

Commenting on Tony Seba in The Telegraph newspaper, journalist Ambrose Evans-Pritchard describes it as "a twin 'death spiral' for big oil and big autos, with ugly implications for some big companies on the London Stock Exchange unless they adapt in time."

As was earlier mentioned, Professor Seba regards the car industry in its current form as already doomed, as it transitions towards the electric self-drive "computer car" of Silicon Valley.

www.bit.ly/2urcXul

MARK CARNEY, Governor of the Bank of England

As Governor of The Bank of England and Chairman of the G20 Financial Stability Board (representing the world's biggest 20 economies, this is an international body that monitors and makes recommendations about the global financial system), Mark Carney is possibly the most highly-regarded figure in the world of international banking.

When he talks, the world listens.

Mr Carney delivered a keynote speech where he talked about the oncoming changes and his words were met with a stunned silence. Read them for yourself:

"The fundamental challenge is, alongside its great benefits, every technological revolution mercilessly destroys jobs and livelihoods – and therefore identities – well before the new ones emerge.

"This was true of the eclipse of agriculture and cottage industry by the industrial revolution, the displacement of manufacturing by the service economy, and now the hollowing out of many of those middle-class services jobs."

His estimation of job loss in the UK alone?
15 million.

www.bit.ly/2umKlfo

A think tank that looked into Mr Carney's figures added that "the necessary digital skills are almost entirely absent from the core curriculum in mainstream schools." They are looking in the wrong place because this learning isn't taking place in the schools. By definition, it has to take place online. Mainstream "ain't where it's at" any more.

ELON MUSK, Creator of Paypal, Owner of Tesla Cars, SpaceX

Elon Musk is as near as you get to a real life Tony Stark. He seems cool, extremely wealthy and a total innovator/visionary. He is, I believe, the most inspirational business leader "out there" and there is no doubting that his ability to think creatively is off the chart, probably equalling the genius of Albert Einstein.

Mr Musk is a leading voice in the growing consensus among CEOs around the world that at a minimum, multiple <u>tens of millions</u> of people are going to lose their jobs and that it will be necessary to implement a UBI (Universal Basic Income). In other words, pay people <u>not</u> to work.

This is the first time that someone is coming up with some kind of a solution and the first time where we begin to look at a change in our working culture. *For the first time in history, we are looking at the possibility that we are making ourselves redundant in the economy that we have created.*

Universal Basic Income is a system in which all citizens receive a standard amount of money each month to cover basic expenses like food, rent and clothes.

In 2016, Elon Musk was quoted to have said at The World Government Summit in Dubai, "I think we'll end up doing Universal Basic Income. It's going to be necessary." He added "There will be fewer and fewer jobs that a robot cannot do better. I want to be clear. These are not things I wish will happen; these are things I think probably will happen."

This was also endorsed by Facebook co-founder, Chris Hughes, among others. Musk continued, "With automation, there will come abundance, almost everything will get very cheap."

Where I struggle with Elon Musk's view is that he seems to be saying that the wealthy elite are _so_ wealthy that their tax bill will in effect pay for everyone else. Call me skeptical, but my belief is that it is precisely their ability to get round (legally) the tax situation that is a part of the problem. There's a guy in the White House who said in a

Presidential debate that he was "smart" because he paid no tax due to a tax loophole and, in the context of tax laws, he's right.

In addition, whilst I see the need for a Universal Basic Income, given that the nature of Governments has consistently been to pay the minimum (and often below the minimum) in payments to its citizens and also given that they are saddled with an ever-increasing level of debt, I do not imagine that the level of UBI will sustain a quality lifestyle, no matter how cheap things become.

www.read.bi/2tQHuAr

PRESIDENT BARACK OBAMA

In the 2016 Economic Report that President Obama gave to Congress, there was a section on the future of robotics in the workforce.

The study was conducted by the White House's Council of Economic Advisers (CEA) and concurred with another report of the American Association for the Advancement of Science (AAAS), as well as the findings of all the previous institutions and individuals mentioned in this book.

In other words, there is a very high chance of massive job losses due to technological advancements. Whilst they all say "may happen", the probability is so high that they might as well be saying "will happen".

The only thing that is different is the percentage of jobs within the American economy that they say will go:

The AAAS estimates 50%. The White House estimates 62%.

March 2017 figures show that the working population in the USA is 160 million. That means that up to 96 million jobs are at risk in the USA alone.

If that isn't enough of a shock for you, the answer to the question "when is this going to happen by?" is frighteningly close. I hope you are sitting down.

Presidents, politicians, international bankers and heads of the leading tech companies in the world all agree that the date the tsunami will hit is ...

2030

<u>Now</u> do you see why I am calling this a tsunami?
Now do you see why I said to Elizabeth in the Post
Office "it's not if but when"?

<u>www.read.bi/2uZjvO3</u>

"It Is Not The Strongest Species That Survive, Nor The Most Intelligent But The Ones Who Are Most Responsive To Change."

Charles Darwin

Chapter 5

So, What Now?

This is the point in my seminars where members of the audience reach the same place as Elizabeth back in the Post Office, with the looks on their faces and questions spinning in their minds. If you are feeling anxious, then understand that this is normal and is why many people don't want to look at this. Stay with it. Now you know what you are dealing with, you can do something about it.

Let's take a "time out" and take on a few points:

1) I am in no doubt that this scenario is on its way, not least because it makes no sense for Mark Carney to be making these statements if it isn't. I take the view that if we prepare for it and it doesn't happen, then either way you will be in a better position. But if it does happen, then you will have saved yourself from a situation that I believe is going to devastate the lives of the millions who do nothing.

Using the tsunami metaphor, right now I'm knocking on your door and pointing out to the horizon and going "er ... guys?" and the purpose of this book is to offer you the "nub" of

20+ years of research so that you can make up your own mind.

2) Recognise that you only have part of the picture, so refrain from making any judgment calls. We have looked at the impact on existing jobs but not what is going on with those who are already "surfing the wave".

   The intention was for you to know how bad it could be for those who choose to do nothing, so that you are clear you need to choose to do something.

3) Manage your state of mind. For many, this process is a shock because it threatens the world that you know. This is part of the reason why I believe that politicians do not stir this particular pot, because they do not want to create alarm on a large scale (because they don't have the answers). I would not be writing this book if I did not believe that the answers are already here.

   In the tsunami of 2004, there is footage of people on the beach completely transfixed by what they were looking at, trying to make sense of it before they realised too late and got swept away. My apologies for the comparison, but right now is where that is most likely to happen and you need to keep on your toes, keep moving. Do not get lost in looking and contemplating for too long.

4) The Deloitte report says that in the past, technological advances have actually resulted in increased employment. So it is not a "given" that the worst-case scenario will occur.

   However, the sheer scale and speed of what is happening, the increased capability of the new technology, the scale on which machines are replacing humans <u>and</u> the fact that the actual nature of businesses is being changed, means that this is not just about the jobs themselves, but that <u>the model of employment</u> itself has to change.

My belief is that the past is no longer a reliable reference point for the future, because it is advancing so fast that it is merging into the present. This is unchartered territory, especially with our ability to process these changes.

The end game, to me, looks like this:

a) There are going to be no areas that are left unaffected. At the very least, the way that people work is going to change in most areas and radically.

b) The worst-case and most likely scenario is job loss on an unprecedented scale.

c) Everyone, from and including senior management downwards, will be hit and the vast majority of mundane jobs will be taken over by robots.

d) Whilst the examples in this book refer mostly to the USA and the UK, this scenario will play out to a greater or lesser extent around the world. In these two economies alone, we could be looking at in excess of 120 million jobs gone by 2030 at the latest. Whilst there will undoubtedly be many millions of jobs that are created, the gap will be massive.

That's 120,000,000 jobs in 13 years.

e) The majority of the remaining jobs will be redefined. We have seen how the responsibilities of the nurse, the truck driver, and the solicitor are all about to be radically changed as technology takes on large and time-consuming areas of their traditional role. The great thing about this is how much time this frees up. However, other aspects such as salary and time spent working will also be redefined. The question is: which way will they go?

f) Niche markets and specialist services will boom and stand out. We are already seeing this in the food area, with companies specialising in high-quality food, specific food types, specialist artisan bakeries and micro-breweries creating their own unique brand of beers.

Also, the internet is seeing the rise of quirky, cool, original businesses being spawned all the time with fresh ideas that captivate the imagination and engage the senses. In the service area, lawyers will move into specialised aspects of law as computers take on the "regular stuff" and accountants will take on specialist tax areas because regular accountancy is performed at the click of a button.

g) Health and wellness will experience unprecedented growth as people seek more solutions to their lifestyle challenges. Nutrition is already experiencing a boom on a scale that is mind-blowing. In addition, where human touch is required (physical therapy), there is limited chance of technology taking over, although having my own chiropractor informs me that there are now machines that can perform manipulations on the spine, having detected the levels of inflammation beforehand!

Care work will also increase as the population makes its biggest demographic shift in our history, with people living to be older.

h) The home-based business will, I believe, be <u>the biggest growth sector of all</u> as the idea of "job 1.0" is redefined and upgraded. This area is, for me, where the real "juice" is because it will offer people real choices over how they spend their time and indeed the lifestyle that they want to experience, that few have had the privilege of living so far.

i) People involved in crafts, real crafts, will also see their businesses grow as the demand for something that has been created and crafted by a human being will gain in demand and also need. Whilst technology is a good thing and it can make life easier in many regards, it also removes our "connection" to reality. Crafts that are creative and serve different functions but "reconnect" the individual to themselves, rather than functioning in an ever-increasing virtual world, are going to be a highly-valued part of people's lives. (If you want an example, then check out www.bit.ly/soundbowls for stunning "musical sculptures", the likes of which you will not have seen.)

j) The class system will dissipate as middle management and below fall into the same general, lower-income bracket, while the distance between the "mega-rich" and the rest increases. The new "class" of billionaires already forms the power base of the future with their financial clout.

Aristocracy be warned ... there is, most definitely, a new sheriff in town.

k) Due to the internet, the actual model of making money will also change. Working online now means that being paid an hourly "time for money" rate is irrelevant. When you can attract thousands of people to pay immediately to your online business, or through (as an example) membership sites, often combined with then paying for a monthly recurring order, a "royalty income" business guarantees a bigger and longer-term payment. This is where the new security is to be found.

l) The internet is not prejudiced. Whatever your gender, sexuality, race, religion or any other form of categorisation, there is no glass ceiling. On the internet, whether you succeed or fail is 100% down to you and the only limitations are your own.

m) Where I hope my own vision is wrong, is the increased number of people falling out the bottom of the net. I would hope that the Universal Basic Income idea would genuinely serve people (it is proving to work in some Northern European countries), but there is the distinct possibility of an "underclass" being created, as is played out in futuristic movies. In some places, it already has and, although I find myself <u>not</u> wanting to write about this, I believe in pragmatic realism, of which this is the gritty part.

There is always a cost to "progress" and this is a part of it.

*   *   *   *   *

So, this is it. This is the tsunami with all of its formidable power.

If you are feeling uncomfortable then I got your attention, which was a necessary requirement. Now we need to look at some of the options that are open to you and the possibilities that they bring.

Before that, let's take another look at the tsunami itself.

Imagine we have had this conversation in person and that now I ask you to come outside and see what I see. If you were to look, you would notice that the wave is still a long way off, close to the horizon, forming an endless continual line.

You would notice a warm sea breeze on your face as you stare into a slight haze, straining your eyes to get a better look as your attention is caught by something appearing on the top of the wave. What was a small point begins to form a straight, white line, right at the top of the wave, moving down and at speed.

"Huh?" is your reaction, as instantly you see another...

As the wave, still a long way off, continues to approach, you think that you hear something through the breeze ... is that shouting? More vertical lines appear going down but now also going across, as the approaching wave is growing in height.

"Is that people yelling out?" You listen more intently and as you hear the sound again, it's clear that it *is* voices and many of them.

Your immediate thought is that they are crying out for help and the sense of alarm increases, but your gut tells you something else.

"What the hell?!" the adrenalin kicks in, but not out of fear: out of excitement. "These guys aren't calling out for help; they're having the time of their lives ... thousands of them."

These guys are surfing the tsunami!

While you might think this exercise over-simplistic, I again emphasise that the <u>pivotal</u> aspect of this book is <u>how</u> you see events unfolding and what you make it mean for you. To be blunt, whether you sink or surf, is <u>entirely</u> your responsibility. Those people who are already surfing the wave? They accept this; in fact they embrace it and have done so not just because the alternative was too awful to contemplate, but in taking on FULL responsibility for creating their lives, they are clear that it will be worth it <u>and</u> that, in every sense, it's the ride of their life.

Best advice? Go find a board.

"It's all about where your mind's at."

Kelly Slate
11 x World Surf League Champion

www.surfingthetechno-tsunami.com

Chapter 6

Tipping Point

Remember the "red pill"? I'm guessing it's kicked in by now.

As we proceed further "down the rabbit hole" and you continue to process this information, I want to bring this all into historical context and, once again, I ask you to stay with this. It's tough going but necessary and by now I'm guessing you recognise this is about the rest of your life.

Around 300 years ago in Britain, the way most people "got by" was making textiles. In those times, people were "crafts folk" and each would make cloth in their cottages - hence the term "cottage industry".

However, it was then realised that if everyone attended a central place of work, efficiencies would be made and so the first factories and mills were created. In that moment, craftsmanship (for the masses) was superseded by manufacturing, the craftsman became the worker and the "industrial" working week was established in its early form. This was when the individual became a cog in a system.

The population collectively bought into the idea of "job security" and began to alter their day-to-day living habits in order to fulfil the requirements of "the job". The "deal" in effect, was to commit personal time (long-term) in exchange for consistent work and a wage (security). "Job 1.0" had been created and it worked. I can imagine that rather than scrabbling around trying to sell your own produce, having someone else paying you a consistent wage must have been a relief. Our basic need for security was satisfied.

Over time, the education system (such as it was) also became a manufacturing process, standardising its lessons and curriculum in order to supply the finished product - the "good" employee.

Fast forward 300 years and "the job" is being squeezed. Salaries that have stagnated over the past 8 years will continue to stagnate, as salaried humans compete with the "free" robots that don't need breaks, shifts, vacation/holidays, or a pension scheme, working 24/7 x 365 means that in many cases there will not be a competition ... and get this, the European Parliament is considering plans to declare them 'electronic persons', with rights!

Mady Delvaux, MEP (Member of European Parliament) said that the European Parliament will vote on proposals within the next 12 months. "This is a new world that we see arriving."

www.dailym.ai/2uhpDnl

If you think this is far-fetched, then rest assured, it's happening already with the added shift in attitude of <u>some</u> businesses adopting a "you should count yourself lucky you have a job" attitude, as they demand subservience.

In many countries, it has been common for a long time for employees not to take their holiday, for fear of appearing "not committed" and no, I am not talking about North Korea.
Out of interest, which country do you think has the <u>least</u> paid vacation time in the world?

Answer: the USA ... interesting huh? It would seem the American dream comes at a cost.

You can expect salaries to be "repackaged" with the basic pay replaced by performance bonuses. In other words, the security is being removed as the income becomes dependent upon results.

As the transition increases, many jobs are not going to be worth having, not if you want to stay sane at any rate. The number of people who are existing in survival mode is tragic, stuck on the hamster wheel, seemingly unable to get off it because they have rent or mortgages to pay and children to take care of. Is it any wonder that the levels of depression and mental illness are on the up?

In the UK it's estimated that there are 14 million people with less than £100 in savings, who are therefore only ever one month away from not being able to pay their mortgage or rent. To live with that constant underlying stress is horrendous and this will undoubtedly be mirrored in the USA, but what is worse is that this is now regarded as normal for so many people.

So why do people stay in this hell? Conditioning. 300 years of an education system designed to make "good employees" produces complacency. If you buy into the job = security "deal" then your brain stops asking questions, literally. It's that simple.

Until now.

We are fast approaching the tipping point, as millions of people are waking up to the "big reveal" that jobs do not equal security, that you cannot compete with something that works for nothing and that the real reward is through working for yourself. Whilst stress and pain is not something to wish upon people, the truth is that it is causing people to wake up and to think for themselves and to ask "what are my options?" NOW people are beginning to ask questions. NOW people are becoming more conscious.

This is <u>huge</u> and is going to be the main driver to a booming home business industry that I have no doubt will impact big time and could even replace Job 1.0 for most people. Once that tipping point is reached, those who make a head start NOW, will make a fortune.

In other words ... the Deal Is Off.

"My passion for surfing was more than my fear of sharks."

Bethany Hamilton-Dirks

(American professional surfer whose left arm
was bitten off in a shark attack and who returned
to - and was victorious in - professional surfing)

www.surfingthetechno-tsunami.com

Chapter 7

The Jedi Strike Back

It is impossible to escape the irony that the very "thing" that is creating the biggest wipeout in terms of jobs (wipeout is also a surfing term) is also the very "thing" that is delivering security on a whole other level.

So the very reason for people settling for Job 1.0 is now being delivered "out there" and with negligible risk. When a "bricks and mortar" business cost a good deal of money to set up, there was a valid reason for being cautious. Now? It's peanuts, so there is no excuse, but there IS this lack of thinking ... which has to be addressed and, once again, is the reason for putting this degree of information in front of you. Most people need to be shocked out of their complacency and also to understand how it came about in the first place.

On one of my mindset courses, I talk about how, "way back when", fleas were trained for flea circuses (stay with me people, this *is* relevant!)

Because a flea can er ... flee, it was necessary to condition them to stay within the "circus", so each flea was placed in a jar and the lid screwed down.

The flea would jump, smacking its head each time, until it would learn to jump just under the height of the lid. Eventually, not only could the lid be taken off and the flea would continue to jump just under the lid height, but when the flea is removed from the jar altogether, it acts as though it's still in the jar.

The parallel is that when we accept from a young age that we will operate within a particular job spectrum with accompanying salary progression over our lifetime, we put our own lid on our own jar, convincing ourselves that we must be "sensible" and "realistic".

One of the beauties of this new world is that "realistic" is whatever you decide it to be. This is why I don't have any expectations for the politicians to come up with the answers, or indeed that our education system is the place to go for future guidance, because both of these institutions are restricted by the past.

This is also why this new wave is so cool, because what fuels it is people's passion for life, for creating something that's exciting and for setting out to be involved with something that is exhilarating in a way that a job can never be.

The days of being reasonable and sensible and stuck in your head are over. The days of wanting to enjoy the ride are here. Finally we are entering an era where what you do on a day-to-day basis is possibly more about who you are Being and less about what you are doing. FAN-BLOODY-TASTIC!

If you want to know where to look, then look to the wave. Look at who is surfing it because these guys have blown the lid off, by thinking outside the box and are making change happen right now, as you read this. Go where the inspiration is and you cannot go wrong.

For example, Elon Musk dares to think outside the box and is challenging old thinking bigger than maybe anyone else out there.

To give you an idea, he has stated that the goals of SolarCity, Tesla, and SpaceX revolve around his vision to change the world and humanity. His goals include reducing global warming through sustainable energy production and consumption, and reducing the "risk of human extinction" by "making life multi-planetary" and establishing a human colony on Mars.

The fact that his Tesla car company has a stock market value greater than Ford, tells you that "the money" believes in him too.

Whereas I suspect Mr Musk is a "one-off", the group to focus on are the guys who are harnessing the power of the internet within their business models.

These are the guys I think of as the rebels, the "Jedi" of the business world, ignoring conventional rules of business as they create invigorating businesses with equally invigorating lifestyles to match. There are a number of similarities that these Jedi knights possess, not least that they all come from "ordinary" backgrounds leading to a no-bullshit attitude, which is totally refreshing.

In addition, the scale of thinking, versatility and speed that they move at, just like surfers reading the wave, darting in and out, looking for that opportunity, can be breathtaking.

In the time that a traditional business will have decided to go with an idea, these guys have come up with an idea, implemented it, tested it and re-tested it before either making it play out or recognising that it was a lame idea and moving on to the next one. The speed of their processing is phenomenal ... which is also why a good number of them speak at a gazillion miles an hour!

You may remember I reported that a think tank that looked into Mr Carney's figures added that "the necessary digital skills are almost entirely absent from the core curriculum in mainstream schools" and that I also said that they were looking in the wrong place ... it's these guys who are the new face of education. Their format is not found in a university lecture theatre but often in a live audience scenario or on a live webinar. Instant!

As a result, they are a band of influencers, busting limitations and cultures wide open, as both men and women emerge with sincere and empowering attitudes. These guys don't just build businesses, they build cultures, using and adapting the power of social media and internet marketing to their advantage, and somewhere within this is where anyone else can make their mark.

As I said, they are transforming traditional ideas into something new and this, in many ways, is what this new wave is all about. What do I mean by that?

Think about it. Is Uber a cab company? Up until it started to use driverless cars, it didn't own any cabs. YouTube hosts the most videos in the world, yet it doesn't make any videos. Facebook, the world's most popular media owner, creates no content. Alibaba, the most valuable retailer, has no inventory. Airbnb, the world's largest accommodation provider, owns no real estate. In each case, the business is not what it seems and the founders have seen a way to use the internet to transform it ... they are surfing the tsunami.

Busting through the barriers that class, sex, colour, education or financial backgrounds put in the way within conventional business, these guys cut to the chase and speak from the heart, using passion, possibility and determination as their currency.

One man at the forefront of this revolution is Gary Vaynerchuk. (www.bit.ly/phpgaryv). He operates out of total integrity and for sure he tells it like it is. Plus, having observed him for a while, I have to catch my breath when I consider how hard he works and this is something I want to flag up from the outset. Whilst the time frames to create this new lifestyle are way shorter than in "Job 1.0", the intensity with which the individual needs to work is increased and consistent. The rewards are greater and so is the responsibility for making it happen. Be mindful of that.

When giving talks to thousands of "vaynerites" (my phrase), he leaves people under no illusion that this isn't a free ride. Whilst his language is often "ripe", I find it totally appropriate with his message. "You need to go where there is opportunity, rather than forcing people to believe in your shit." and "My level of giving a fuck whether you believe what I am saying, is zero." were just two of his choice phrases I listened to when he gave a Q&A session in London.

This guy lives with his heart on his sleeve and takes no prisoners. To be honest, it's what we need right now, as people take a reality check.

Welcome to the new Rock and Roll!

"'Your time is limited, so don't waste it living someone else's life."

Steve Jobs

Chapter 8

Pick Your Wave

As we look at an overview of some of the different business options that are right now producing great results, it is common to put "financial provisos" in sections and talk about "not typical earnings" etc.

I'm not going to do that. Instead I am just going to make a different statement ... if your intention in a new business is to make it work, not "to see" if you can make it work, or to just dip your toe in the water to take the temperature ... or anything other than 100% commitment to making it work at any cost, then you need to focus on becoming self-aware, so you can ensure you are aligned with your stated intention.

I had a client who was telling me all the right things about his business and that he was committed to reaching certain targets at a specified time. I was checking out his body language as he was speaking. Something wasn't right. So at the end of his "I'm gonna make it happen" speech, I simply asked ... "Are you sure?" to which he said "Yes". I said nothing and allowed the silence to prompt him to add" ... and if I don't, I'll be devastated."

Did you see it?

Right there is exactly the kind of subtle "get-outs" in your thinking that you need to be aware of. Being single-minded is to have only one point in your mind and in this case that is the successful achievement of a goal. If there is an additional "if I don't then ... " then your mind is not only <u>not</u> focused on making it happen, but has already created a back door out, with the added stench of the smell of burning martyr.

One of the things that frustrates me (putting it politely) is the number of people who go around calling themselves an entrepreneur when, in fact, they are merely playing at it; and then justify their failure because of all sorts of reasons.

What is truly bizarre is that some people "get off" from playing the wounded hero scenario, rather than the victor. Make no mistake: business is tough and to go through all that crap in return for being an almost-ran is not worth it - not for you and not for your family.

So rather than a "wealth warning", I am instead stating categorically that you need to take complete responsibility for what you are focusing on, ensure it's on what you truly and powerfully want, <u>and</u> commit. This will, ultimately, lead you to success. If you look at all those who fail and all those who succeed, they contain different mindsets with different habits and <u>it starts with the intention.</u>

If you have any doubt, then get coaching, do whatever it takes until you are sure. Everyone who has succeeded has had to go through a baptism of fire to give up on old patterns, often in the face of intense pressure to quit. So, get your mind set before you start.

Once you make a statement as to what it is that you want, Life will step up, slap you round the face, bring up all your negative beliefs and doubts, look you in the eye and ask "Are you absolutely sure?" ... then most likely slap you again and wait for your answer. If you disappear back into doubt, then it will smother you in remorse. If you take a step forward, look Life full in the face, laugh and tell it you don't answer to anyone other than you, then it will stand aside and let you through.

On a final note, these guys allow themselves to be unfettered in their thinking to the point that they inspire themselves into playing a phenomenal game. They don't care at all what others think and respond only to how good it feels to be doing what they are doing. They follow their own internal compass.

The game has to be phenomenal to make going on this journey worthwhile. So, allow your imagination to play full out with regards to the possibilities and expect your logical side to want to keep it in check ... and tell it that it's no longer in charge.

Your <u>feelings</u> are going to play the key role in directing you ... they have to because it is impossible to be inspired and feel nothing.

"Select waves by looking out to the horizon. Pick a wave that is further out. Do not rush and decide to catch a wave when it is only one metre in front of you. Give yourself time to prepare yourself."

Surfing Magazine

www.surfingthetechno-tsunami.com

Internet Marketing

Internet marketing is the blanket term for the majority of processes on the internet, aimed at creating awareness through marketing in all its multiple forms and ultimately to generate new business.

The ability of the internet to relay information to 50% of the world's population (<u>3.8 billion</u> people) has fuelled the entrepreneurial revolution and transforms the destructive power of the tsunami into the most creative power the world has ever known. To put it in perspective, a smart phone contains more power than NASA's entire computing capability that put a man on the moon. The sky is no longer the limit.

Internet marketing is the domain of the pure entrepreneur, where marketing skills and the ability to think from a creative perspective are the tools to deploy. Combine a sharp marketing strategy with a great product and the financial reward can be fast and massive.

There are multiple processes that are used (which is why looking out for a <u>reputable</u> marketing college is imperative) but the general idea is to attract multiple thousands of responses into an automated system that communicates with the potential purchaser at each stage of their "experience" and results in multiple purchases.

Once a customer base is established then other offers are introduced to what is now a "friendly" market, resulting in further sales and most often increasing in value. This is known as "upselling" and is where significant sums are made.

The effortlessness of a fully-automated system, combined with the sheer size of the internet. makes creating a streamlined business possible. Increasingly, and incredibly, companies receive no phone calls regarding their product, with the whole marketing process being carried out online. This is remarkable.

HOWEVER, stating the obvious, you <u>have</u> to have an idea that works, so if you are not an "ideas person" and/or if you are not willing to learn, create, test and recreate entire new processes then this isn't your wave. Recognise this and move on; there are others.

Be aware of the following, just so your feet are on the ground when making any choices:

Whilst the allure of making a "big strike" is powerful, the likelihood is that you will have several smaller successes that combined will lead you to success.

With any business, you need to invest time and money into studying and implementing various different projects until one begins to take hold. Compared to a conventional business model, the sums required can be insignificant, but nonetheless take this on as a requirement.

If you are starting out with no experience, then be prepared to process a lot of information. My own experience has been to stagger out from these courses with a sense of being punch drunk, as I am someone who gets easily overwhelmed, so I have to pace myself.

Check out Simon Coulson and The Internet Business School in the "Author's Recommendations" section towards the back of the book. I have got to know Simon over the past couple of years and the calm understatement with which he gives his talks and coaching hides one of the most focused and active minds in business that I have had the good fortune to come across.

Take note that his background is totally "normal"; no privileged education or money are behind him. It was his frustration stuck as a Customer Service Manager in a telecoms company that drove him to massively succeed in internet marketing and to go on to create the pre-eminent businesses in Internet Marketing Education in Europe.

In addition, he very much lives his dream. With a passion for music, this guy has played to a sell-out O2 arena in London as well as now owning a music writing company (generated online of course) that enables him to hang out with a whole group of number one hit songwriters at HIS songwriting academy. Simon is the classic example of how you don't have to wait until you retire to get out and live your dreams. He incorporates it as a daily part of his considerable business empire.

Creating an online membership

One business format many companies benefit from is the membership site. Remember we have talked about using different financial models and, without a doubt, using one whereby people need to pay a monthly subscription or a regular payment for a monthly product has massive benefits.

So a membership site is one of those models that as well as creating a "tribe", has the added bonus of generating ongoing residual income, as the membership fees are paid monthly.

Of course it's great to secure upfront purchases; the consistency and security of a long-term membership platform cannot be underestimated. To <u>know</u> that your monthly outgoings are underpinned for the foreseeable future gives a true sense of liberty from the grind.

One of my favourite examples of seeing an opportunity with an existing problem and using the internet to create a whole new business came from a couple of guys who jointly took on running their two sons' soccer team.

Having discovered that it wasn't just meeting up for a kick about as they had to sort out kit, fixtures, insurance, police checks, health and safety, equipment and a training diary, they recognised they had to do something about it to make it easier.

When they realised that at their club alone, there were five other teams and that they could add other clubs in their town, county and country, it became apparent they had a market of tens of thousands, all of who would save time, money and hassle. So they created a membership site with all the information <u>and suppliers</u> for each organiser of each team.

The membership fees for this one site generate over £1 million per annum!

If you have an idea for creating one then this would be a highly effective wave to catch for sure. If you don't ... keep on paddling out.

Affiliate Marketing

One of the most straightforward ways of starting out is affiliate marketing. You don't need your own idea because you can market someone else's and take a commission on any sales.

The process is similar to that of internet marketing. You look to attract thousands of responses in order to take them through to a point where a percentage will buy.

If you get this right, you will benefit from a very healthy financial return, with the advantage of it being fully automated and so freeing up your time, creating a definite quality of life. No rat-race, no commute, money coming in.

Many people start "apprenticing" in this area before going on to do their own thing, because you learn as you earn, so it gets you "on the court". If this suits your personality type, perhaps this is the one, but before you get carried away by the potential reward, recognise your own learning style. If you don't like solitary learning, I would suggest this is not for you.

Affiliate marketing is quite a "clinical" process in that it is for the sole purpose of generating income. If you are motivated by money alone, then you will have no problem with affiliate marketing, but often people need more than "just money".

Building an online Amazon business

A category within affiliate marketing that has evolved into its own niche is how to create a retail business through Amazon. The reach of this truly remarkable business model now means that people are successfully using the power and versatility of Amazon to run their own business through. The nub of this is to find or create a product and promote it, harnessing yourself to the power of Amazon who acts as your market place and distribution outlet. The simplicity of this model and its ability to utilise the power of this giant in the industry is wonderfully simple.

For both Affiliate and Amazon marketing, once again check out Simon Coulson in "Author's Recommendations", as these are areas that are taught within his curriculum having been <u>highly</u> successful at them himself.

Becoming an Author

Do you have what it takes to write a book?

For most people, there is a straightforward answer to this question. However, before you come to a quick 'no', have a think about it. When I say 'write a book,' I am not talking about fiction. I'm talking about writing a 'how-to' type book, which teaches people a certain skill or process. Let me explain the benefits of this:

Firstly, if you are looking at the idea of marketing a business from a different angle, then writing a book could be something for you to consider. This book is an example of how educating people, and placing information in front of them, can lead to people making positive choices. Personally, I believe that the sheer satisfaction of holding your own published book in your hands provides one of the most rewarding experiences you can have.

Secondly, if you have something unique to share, then that could be the basis for writing your book. If your book has a particular purpose that it serves, then again, that is a really good reason to write one. Send your message out to the world; let them hear what you have to say!

Now, let me tell me you a little bit about the publication business:

The introduction of digital printing, and of course, the ability to sell (and print) via Amazon has transformed this business. When I wrote and self-published my first book, I had to order a print run of one thousand copies, just to get the print costs down to a reasonable level.

Nowadays, print on demand means that you can order one book at a time, and it will be printed and sent straight out to the customer. In other words, it's all done in-house. Whilst this means that you make slightly less money per copy, there is no exposure to risk, or the need to carry stock. Amazing! In addition, it is now possible to launch a book on Amazon in an instant. This means that the platform from which to sell your book is literally just one click away.

There are a number of courses out there on how to write and publish your own book, but I urge you to be cautious. It is very easy for your ego to be massaged with the line that "we all have a book in us" and whilst that may be true, it might not be a book that anyone else wants to buy. Some of these courses cost a HUGE sum ($40,000+) but there is one that I recommend. The cost of this course is but a fraction of the above, and the information is the most detailed and up to date you could wish for.

Check out Richard McMunn in the "Author's Recommendations" section, both for the content of his courses and his prices, which are, without a doubt, value for money.

Richard's story of how he created a £5 million+ publishing business, having started out as a fireman, is yet further testimony to the fact that you do not need formal training in these areas.

Clearly, writing a book requires you to have an idea and also the patience to write a book (tell me about it!)

If you don't have either, then most definitely this isn't your wave.

Property

In many countries, owning and developing property has for a long time been considered a sound way to create a solid income.

However, if your perception is that you need a lot of money to get started, that it is a big risk or that you simply don't know how to go about it, then there is one person in the UK that you need to consider, who has removed these obstacles.

In addition, he used impressive internet marketing strategies to create a real presence, by doing something that he loves, which is teaching others how to do the same. So, whilst at the point of writing I have not personally attended his seminars, the reason I have no hesitation in recommending him, in addition to the impressive testimonials, is because I have met him on several occasions, witnessed his rise in the market place and seen how he has grown and matured into an impressive individual.

He was courageous enough to feature in a BBC documentary where, as the owner of a property, he went to live in place of a tenant of his for one week and off her budget. His whole approach was to be open to learning and improving right from the start and it was clear he found the whole process fascinating, whilst owning up to areas he had not been aware of. You don't open yourself up to that level of scrutiny, unless you truly believe in what you are doing.

So, if the notion of owning several properties and deriving income and long-term security as a strategy is of interest to you, then check out Paul Preston in the Author's Recommendations section, for his free one-day Property Investment Fast Track courses. As with all these options, check in with yourself as to whether this is something that on a "gut level" appeals, because it requires, as do they all, your time and attention in order to make it work.

On the "upside", you do not need to be creative or to have your own business idea because it's about following a particular process. It also gives you a residual income, backed up by an appreciating asset (i.e. the property should go up in value) so once in place, it is a long-term solution and that enables you to be freed up in life.

To cover a potential "downside", I would consider that whilst property can clearly be a solid and highly profitable investment, if you get it wrong, then you might go through a great deal of effort and make some costly mistakes ... e.g. wrong house, area or tenants ... so getting educated from someone with Paul's experience and formula is essential and avoids that.

Check out Paul in the "Author's Recommendations" section to see the value he gives.

Social Media Marketing

The world of social media marketing is, without doubt, exhilarating in its power, its immediacy and its reach. This is the playground for those who want to make an impact, create a brand and in some regards, change the world. It can be fast paced and one hell of a ride and it can also be unforgiving too, as the amount of traffic increases on a daily basis with more and more people looking to get noticed above the ever-increasing noise.

With some people specialising in communicating on one platform, whilst others teach how to create a portfolio spread of communication across many, there is one guy who I again wholeheartedly recommend for a number of reasons.

The first is that he has gone and done it big time and has created a number of different businesses and, along the way, multiple 7-figure incomes. The second is because when I first had the luck of sitting in on one of his presentations, I could not help grinning almost all the way through, because of his infectious sense of sheer joy at what the science of social media enables people to do ... whilst he was in mid flow, his own sense of excitement and genuine joy at what he was showing us was possibly the most refreshing experience I have had as a course participant.

The third reason is because he, like myself, has a whole personal development ethos that accompanies his business, which in some ways is the most important thing (for both of us) because THAT is where the real teaching occurs.

I have said that this all begins and ends in the mind and I am comfortable with the idea that we are both in full agreement on that principle. This guy's name is Ed J C Smith and, once again, he lives his dreams right alongside his work. In fact, I would suggest they are fully interchangeable.

On one of the many conversations that Ed and I have shared, when I asked him why he did what he did and got so much enjoyment out of it, he thought for a moment and then, grinning, said "I just love people!" Now, I am a cynic when most people say something like this but having done the kind of coaching that I have for as long as I have, I like to think I am a good judge of body language and in Ed's case, I had no doubt. The guy positively shines.

Once again, go check out the "Author's Recommendation" section to find out more about Ed.

Event Marketing

If you like the idea of setting up your own event, whether it's a live course or exhibition, then the events market is a hugely rewarding one to step into. There is a unique buzz to this industry due to the fact that it's live and entails lots of people getting together.

There is actually not too much to say about it, because if you are into this and your business model requires it, then that's all there is to deciding. However, once again, there is the matter of how you promote a successful business event and there is only one person in the UK who I wholeheartedly recommend. His name is Nick James and his company is called SeriouslyFunBusiness ... check him and his company out.

As with all these guys, whilst he genuinely has fun, this guy has come out of lots of mistakes, lots of ups and downs, like us all, and from a typical background that gave no clue as to his destination ... and he works his butt off.

There are some sound reasons for checking this guy out and I have no hesitation in giving him a 100% endorsement ... here's why:

1) I have been on his "Bums on Seats" course (cool title!) and observed his teaching style as authentic and totally honest; this guy over delivers and at too little a price.

The level of his thinking and detail goes beyond anything I have done before, but also he shares information about his own company and how he breaks down costs, profit etc.

2) This guy also puts on his own events and he walks his talk. Earlier in the book, I have mentioned Gary Vaynerchuk, who is *the* thought leader of social media marketing with a real rock and roll following. Nick had one conversation with this guy, who decided in an instant to come to London for the first time ever and be at Nick's own event, in front of a sell-out crowd as the headline "act".

   It was an event I consider myself to be lucky to have attended, not just to listen to Gary V's profound observations but to see Nick on stage, trying to handle that his biggest dream had not only come true but that he was in it too! A great moment!

If this terrifies you, or seems to be a lot of hassle then, once again, this is not your wave ... there's more.

Network Marketing

Credit must be given to the industry that has introduced <u>hundreds of millions</u> of ordinary people (no exaggeration) to the idea that there is an alternative to Job 1.0. and has inspired millions to choose a different path and to create lifestyles that were totally "off the radar" until that point: lifestyles that are, in many instances, jaw dropping!

In addition, this industry has played an unsung role in introducing personal development and mindset as a core part of a progressive culture.

The principle idea behind Network Marketing is to endorse a company because you're a fan of its products and to then create a business (distributorship) from marketing the products and the business opportunity itself. Over time, others become distributors within your group and repeat the process, then a network of marketers develops (hence the industry name.)

The power of this business model is that as each distributor is building their own business, they are also building yours, resulting in a small profit being generated from everything that their business sells. It's like opening up mini franchises of which you are the franchise holder.

Over time, the network of distributors grows into the many thousands, locking in a long-term residual "walk away" income, underpinned by the combination of a self-motivated group of business

owners and products that most typically are
reordered monthly, thus creating a repeated
monthly income.

There are several upsides to this industry: it
provides a ready-made "off the peg" solution <u>and</u>
the startup cost is negligible. (In fact and in all
seriousness, it's too cheap.)

Also, because it's in the interest of the person
whose business you are a part of to support you, it
can be a true win/win, as you are part of a team as
well as creating your own.

The social aspect is a really important factor here.
For many people, the reason they <u>won't and
shouldn't</u> do the previous-mentioned options is
because social engagement is the difference
between loving something and being miserable. I
don't care how much money you "might" earn, a)
you most likely won't earn much if you are
miserable and b) the whole point is that you no
longer need to compromise your soul! Why be
miserable when you could be pouring your heart
into something else ... so ok, you might make
"only" £25k a month rather than £32k a month but
feeling miserable for an extra £7k (especially at
that level) is too high a price to pay.

If working with other people matters to you, this could be your wave.

The downsides are that often the culture many of these companies use is outdated, hyped-up rhetoric, relying on "sales type" techniques to cover over a business of little substance, resulting in people feeling hassled by a cheap, amateur approach, many of whom are friends and family! Not good!

In addition, the terminology is often really dated. Terms such as "making a prospect list" straight away dehumanise people, which for a people business is nuts! If anyone calls you up asking "for your opinion on something", then straight away they are manipulating. It's not necessary and you can see it a mile off. If you do this, then stop. It's not necessary.

When choosing a company, the first question to ask yourself is "do I see this business thriving in 15 years' time?" Gut feel. If the answer is no, then don't go near it.

Another aspect that some people find tough is that you need to be proactive in finding people to talk to. If this is not a skill you are willing to learn, then this is not your wave.

There are some really great companies out there and if you are looking for one, then make sure it stands for something other than making money. What does it pride itself on? Look for a company mission statement and notice whether it's talked about or whether people are only talking about the money they make. If the company has any kind of integrity, then its mission statement should run through its core.

Also, look to see the professionalism of the distributors. If their motivation is the satisfaction of helping others (by definition not ego-based), then it's a clear indication that the company values are in line with theirs. You are left in no doubt when you have come across a professional network marketer, because you feel as though you have been really listened to, which is rare in this day and age.

One such person I have had the good fortune to get to know, who constantly demonstrates these qualities whilst making around an eight-figure fortune, is Steve Mitchell.

In my coaching, I am always fascinated why people continue beyond the point where, financially, they need to and when I asked Steve this question, the frustration in his eyes at an "unfinished job" was a complete surprise and told me his answer was sincere:

"I've helped thousands to create better lifestyles but I haven't helped nearly enough people to build truly <u>phenomenal</u> lifestyles and I won't be satisfied until I have helped a significant number of deserving people to achieve this."

Legacy in business is a powerful driver.

Steve has yet another inspiring story of someone who faced the possibility of bankruptcy when his restaurant business got hit in a recession and then he was introduced to network marketing.

Once again, with no background in this business, it was his attitude that counted (getting the hint yet?!). With consistent energy, drive, passion and hard work, coupled with a clear business mind, he demonstrates, along with all the others featured in this chapter, all the reasons why he will undoubtedly create a legacy to be proud of. But it's not just because of his achievements that he features in this book, it's because he works sincerely and modestly, supporting others in establishing the same level of success, driven by a real mission that I find singularly impressive.

* * * * *

As you have seen in this chapter, there is an array of options, each one of which is delivering fantastic results for individuals who have taken the plunge, worked their butt off and liberated themselves from their previous mundane and stressed Job 1.0 existence to a lifestyle that was inconceivable before.

But there is one key distinction between Job 1.0 and any of these options that you also need to be willing to take on fully, that may seem obvious for many but needs to be addressed. Have you ever had a real chat with yourself in the mirror? No? Well ... there's always a first time.

"The intuitive mind is a sacred gift and the rational mind is a faithful servant.
We have created a society that honours the servant and has forgotten the gift."

Albert Einstein

www.surfingthetechno-tsunami.com

Chapter 9

Note To Self ...

OK, so remember when I said that this book was for entrepreneurs and non-entrepreneurs? That's this bit.

Like everything in this book, I am making you aware so your decisions are well-informed ones. Preparation and the correct choice at this stage can save you months/years of stress and money, so I'm giving you a reality check. This is where you need to check in with yourself and have that "talk in the mirror" in order to get ready to take yourself on.

Many of my clients notice that transitioning from employee to entrepreneur takes a shift in thinking, moving from "hoping that someone would tell them what to do" to stepping up and owning the whole process. Often, this is the final barrier before stepping fully across the threshold of being a business owner/entrepreneur and it can happen to those in the highest of positions.

An amusing example is when, after being elected as Pope, Pope John Paul II commented "for the first few months I kept on hearing myself say 'I must go and ask the Pope' and then I would jolt myself with the realisation: hang on ... I <u>am</u> the Pope!"

In any Job 1.0, focus and application is required. However, <u>unlike</u> any Job 1.0, when creating your own business, the key difference is that <u>you</u> are the one who has to create the vision, hold the vision and who is responsible for <u>everything</u>. In the early days in particular, there is no leaving work behind at the end of the day. If it's not consuming you, you're not doing it right, because your mind will continue to throw up different thoughts all the time and you have to go with that.

You must be "willing to do whatever it takes". If you aren't willing to be in that place, don't even begin, simply because if you start to shut down your flow of thought by telling yourself, "This isn't work time", then your mind interprets this as meaning it's not a priority, that your maximum creativity isn't required. Then your brain will work at reduced levels and will deliver something that is not your best. Why do that? Mediocre is what's killing most people.

Whilst there are huge rewards, you have to discipline your mind and actions to make it happen and having the mental strength to lead yourself when you will inevitably get challenged is essential.

This is about your character and bringing a new game to the court. Don't turn up at the "metaphorical gym" saying you want to create a strong body and then complain because the weights are all heavy! Accepting it's going to be both tough and rewarding gets your mind on your side.

Once again, it depends on how you choose to see this, but to have the opportunity to take yourself on, for fantastic rewards and a strong sense of self-worth ... in fact to BECOME someone you truly admire, has got to be what it's all about, hasn't it?

The reason why I'm spending this time pointing this out is because estimates indicate that there are going to be tens of millions of people who are going to have to look to something radically different in order to make a living.

In addition, we have to face the "elephant in the room" that most people who are writing about entrepreneurship are failing to address, which is this ...

Most people don't want to be an entrepreneur!

... and with tv shows like "The Apprentice" implying you have to stab everyone in the back, sell your soul to "get to the top" and become an all-round gross and offensive individual, I am not surprised that this is the case. The new era heralds people being mutually respectful and having a far higher level of interpersonal skills as well. The days of the emotionally-illiterate male, I sincerely hope, are on the decline.

The next chapter talks about the option that my own business specialises in. If you haven't yet identified with any of the previous options, my guess is that you need something that gives you more in terms of support and less in terms of needing to create an idea of your own and designing and building an entire business model from scratch.

I want to address another reality. Having made the decision to explore the world of online business, it has required me to spend a great deal of time and tens of thousands of pounds in the process. Along the way, I have sat through multiple courses whilst wanting to throw my laptop out of the window in frustration.

I am well aware that I get overwhelmed with this kind of learning and it's been tough ... in fact, it still is. I want it all done for me!! So, I've been in the trenches whilst being fortunate in that I am able to afford the time to do so.

The reality I want to address is that there are increasing numbers of people who are working harder, commuting longer and getting paid less, dealing with increasing levels of stress and arriving back home, stressed and exhausted and truthfully having no inclination or energy to suddenly step into "entrepreneur mode".

On top of which, they often have family commitments as well and need to "be there" for their family.

When I coach my clients, we look at willpower and how it gets weakened with each new project in our life requiring our attention. To create a business that works, you need to be able to focus intently on it, not have it as one of many things going on in your life.

So, with everything else people have to contend with, there is very little "juice left in the battery" to have an original idea and to go out and create it.

In fact, the ideal solution for most people is to <u>not</u> have to be an entrepreneur, <u>not</u> have the stress of coming up with (and fully testing) their own idea, but instead to be able to plug into an already-existing, fully-tested, "plug and go" online business.

What would be even better, would be to have a fully defined role, so that the individual knows what their areas of responsibility are and what skill sets they need to develop.

Furthermore, they need to know that what they are getting involved with offers the chance to grow and develop on their terms AND provides all the rewards on offer from the entrepreneurial world, without needing to hassle people, friends and family to manipulate them into a business.

In other words, pick out all the best bits of all the different models we've just looked at and combine them with the social benefits of Job 1.0 and the off-the-chart rewards, security and liberty that being an entrepreneur offers, without any of the risk.

That's not too much to ask, is it?!

Not at all.

Welcome to Job 2.0.

"Never doubt that a small group of committed citizens can change the world: Indeed it's the only thing that ever has."

Margaret Mead

www.surfingthetechno-tsunami.com

Chapter 10

Integrated Marketing

I believe that Integrated Marketing could become bigger than all the other options we have looked at combined. The reason is very simple. As more and more people are moving out of the workplace and into self-employment, there are two aspects that will defino whether someone stays stuck or makes the move: 1) Time and 2) Money.

Integrated marketing takes both of these issues out of the equation.

It also upgrades and redefines the concept of Job 1.0 into Job 2.0, where the individual truly gets the best of both the job and the entrepreneur, without needing to be either employed or needing to create, test, fund and implement their own idea. But here's the best bit ... it enables people with no ideas of their own, and also people who are "time and money restricted". to step into a ready-made business model that enables them to have an entire online business up and running, with strong foundations for future years ahead, in a staggeringly quick timeframe.

In addition, combining aspects of business models you have already read about, results in needing an almost incomprehensibly <u>low</u> number of customers in order to establish a solid base for a business that will continue to pay out bonuses into the long-term future. So many businesses being created will only be around for the short-term (i.e. 3 years at most?), which means that many people will have to build all over again ... this makes no sense if the intention is to create long-term security.

Integrated Marketing is so called because its participants use and endorse the company's products or services in their day-to-day life (i.e. they are integrated into their lifestyle.) It is because people are influenced by and trust what their friends/peers say, that companies are sitting up and taking notice. This is where the whole notion of "job" is being redefined.

The culture is very different in that it's focused on intelligently using all the "smart bits" of social media marketing in a "point and click" online process, focusing on initially educating the audience, so that there is no chasing or hassling involved. Instead, your customers respond to your social media approach. A skill set of being able to post on social media gets you started but, like any job, <u>you must</u> have a willingness to learn and progress.

There is no need to spend the thousands of pounds/dollars and considerable time and overwhelm on courses, because there are defined responsibilities (like a job spec) and a process for setting up and establishing your "online, franchise-style business", in order to benefit from rewards that are off the scale compared with most salaried jobs.

In addition, there are opportunities for further personal and business growth. For many people, this aspect of being in a business that encourages supporting your business through effectively supporting others and creating a strong connection between people, is as important as the financial side. In an era where the levels of depression, isolation and mental illness are massively on the increase, to have a business with a social conscience is a rare commodity.

The real beauty of this model lies in that it turns basic principles of internet marketing on their head.

In all other internet marketing options, you need to attract thousands in order to sell and up-sell to them (i.e. sell them a low ticket item and then go on to sell higher and higher ticket items until you have no more to sell to that group and so you have to repeat the process.)

With the Integrated Marketing model, to create a walk-away, residual income, the amount of customers you need to attract (out of the 2 billion people on Facebook) is ...

30!

"Huh?"

Yup, that's right. 30.

And you only need to get them the once. No repeat marketing for more and more customers and no up-selling.

Amazing, right?

How this works is that the customer isn't just purchasing from your product line. In essence they are buying their own online store.

Here is where it gets even better.

When those 30 people take on promoting their own online stores (kind of like them buying an online franchise from you), two things happen. The first is that you get a percentage override on all the business each "franchise" generates.

This isn't "money for nothing" as you have a duty to support them until they create their own levels of competence, but it's not what I would define as "hard work". The cool thing is: who wouldn't be motivated to make sure all the franchise-style businesses you introduce are set up right, if you are going to make an ongoing residual income from them? Just as McDonalds train their franchise holders to create an effective business, so will you. When you then realise that this largely consists of "checking in" with these guys, to see what help they need and ensure that they are enrolled on the appropriate course, you begin to see how simple this process is.

The second thing is that, with most companies, the bonus reward structure means that when those 30 people market and attract others to do the same, your business begins to form a group of mini online franchises, none of which are in competition with each other. Companies are waking up to this and recognizing that rather than paying a superstar £$ 80 million, it makes far more sense to incentivise people like you and me to promote their products.

What then happens is that as consistent sales are made throughout the group, on top of the bonuses, you receive a regular, ongoing, dependable monthly commission, giving you long-term and predictable income/profit.

This is where you access real marketing power, because you can have a massive budget promoting your overall business in a way that cannot be matched in any other model, with <u>minimal</u> cost to you.

Watch this:

These are average figures for the amount people spend on internet/social media marketing in relation to what they earn per year (£/$/€ it's pretty much the same).

<u>Internet/Social Media Marketing:</u>

Advertising Spend (per month)	Turnover (up to)
£$500-1k	£$100k
£$2k-10k	£$500k
£$30k-50k	£$1 million +

<u>Integrated Marketing:</u>

You spend £$400 a month.

Month 1
If you generate 20 integrated marketers who spend £$400 a month:

20 x £$400 = £$8k / month
+ your £$400 / month = £$8.4k / month

This is the overall marketing budget spent by everyone within your group on their businesses and therefore your business.

Month 2
If your 20 integrated marketers have also got 20 integrated marketers who have now opened their own online stores and let's say that you don't do any further marketing for that month:

20 x 20 x £$400 = £$160,000 / month

Even if you slash these figures drastically, you still, within a couple of months, end up having an overall marketing budget of someone making £$1 million a year.

And you are still spending (maybe) £$400 a month.

When you then add this power and combine it with the fact that you are focusing on low numbers, it makes a winning combination and means there is room for everyone. This takes away the need to compete, leaving you to focus on supporting your whole business, and on sincere heartfelt communication with living breathing <u>people</u> who have similar wants and needs to you.

2 billion people on Facebook and you are looking for 30? The difference is that this is the entire culture of Integrated Marketing; there is no need for the "frenzied" approach that is so often driven by mindlessness and greed.

With many outdated business models, there is this "sling enough mud at the wall and some of it will stick" attitude, which tells you that the thinking is too haphazard.

With Integrated Marketing, right from the start you set out to create a measured, professional business that is totally dedicated to achieving your goals, through supporting others to do the same, creating something that collectively gives you and your colleagues security for the rest of your lives.

I knew this was a winner, because each time I talked this through with any of the internet marketing experts, on every occasion, they recognised that this was something new, not just in stats but in attitude and approach.

It was out of these conversations that I created The Mellow Marketing Company, with the strap line "...because Life isn't meant to be stressful", because this is how I passionately believe we should be living our lives.

What each individual makes from this varies, because there are many different factors as well as different personal motivations. But this gives the average person the most authentic chance, with support, of stepping up into a totally different level of income and quality of life. The fact that it's royalty-based (because every one of your mini franchise-style business holders is buying each month from their stores, which are all in YOUR business), means that you have built-in, long-term, walk-away residual income.

Interestingly, Richard Branson commented in a recent interview that if he was to start over, this is the model he would use.

It's also interesting, looking at Branson and Virgin as an example, because it shows you how favourable the Integrated Marketing model is compared to the more "conventional" business structure (and I take nothing away from the man; he's a complete inspiration).

Branson has around 500 businesses and for each one of them he will have recruited a CEO, with Branson most likely the Chairman. Those CEOs will then have their own board of directors who will have their junior directors / vice presidents. They in turn will have their own "minions" and departments, who will have more people, until you get to the basic level of employment, resulting in Virgin employing (probably) hundreds of thousands of people all over the world. Everyone, even in a modern company like Virgin, will be in their Job 1.0 jar.

Branson is the one guy who gets the cream (I have no problem with that, it's his creation) but no one can go above him.

The beauty of Integrated Marketing is that you can get involved today and overtake everyone, if that's "your driver". The reality is that with this system, the only limits are those you set in your mind.

"Great things in business are never done by one person. They're done by a team of people."

Steve Jobs

Another real beauty about this process is the mindset behind it, in that you start by getting 100% clear on what matters to you, in <u>YOUR</u> life. How often do you get to do that? Most people are caught up in living within a permanent reaction, rather than taking a step back and actually asking themselves "What matters to me?" and "How do I want to live my life?"

Once you have that clear, you then look at the payment plan of the business and understand what levels of the plan deliver what it is you want. This forms the core of your personal plan and a strategy as to how to reach it. (In Mellow Marketing, we teach "sat nav planning" so that people recognise this really is a journey with a route, a destination and a desired end result.)

Then, further understand that this is to give you <u>the choice</u> of stepping off whilst your business continues to generate income. Having the choice is what gives you freedom. Whether you take it is also your choice.

Once you have that clarity about what matters to you, from that moment on, your entire focus is on assisting others in doing exactly the same. People power personified.

You then begin operating within a business model and authentically supporting others to grow, opening them up to new possibilities and transforming "work" into a rich social and personal growth path. This is the real power behind this business and from where a profound sense of satisfaction is generated. I believe there is nothing more powerful than when people proactively support each other.

In fact, as "formulas" go, there is no other model this powerful. It's precisely because it's a culture about people, prosperity and a positively challenging environment that means it's not just about creating a business, it's about creating a movement. Most people will do far more for a cause and for others than they will for themselves. This change of focus is what generates something special and well-intentioned, as it is aimed at getting people out of the way of the tsunami and fully mobile in the new economy. My time coaching the top teams in the English Premier League showed me that when you have a group of individuals playing for the team, something very powerful happens that simply cannot occur when individuals only think about themselves.

This model establishes its own independent economy, creating security, regardless of what is going on in the rest of the world. The end result is a quality of life free from the stresses and associations that Job 1.0 was completely vulnerable to. Be clear in this ... everyone is aware that they are all working together and therefore there is individual accountability, but if you are getting this level of support, why would you not want to play ball?

I made the statement at the beginning of the book that I consider that we are witnessing the beginnings of a new era in our civilisation and this is very much a part of it.

Work is now being redefined, not just in terms of how we make money, but the amounts of it and the time freedom it gives us. This is a social revolution, backed up by economic prosperity and underpinned by people growing and feeling good, proud and clear about who they are and supporting their fellow builders in the process. The combination of people AND technology is essential and this is where if there were any caution on many of the other options, it is that they largely involve sitting in front of a computer without the personal, live interaction. While technology and the internet bring many huge advantages, it is important to be aware that getting hooked on it can cause isolation and depression.

One of the ironies of Facebook is that whilst people can have hundreds of "friends" on there, it is already being demonstrated that more and more people are depressed as a result. We are now in the bizarre age when people spend a whole load of time and effort to portray a virtual image that increasingly others regard as real when it's not. It's a virtual identity that people are believing is real.

With this model, reality is in the connection between people and their support for each other and their commitment. I have a saying in my business: "I am more committed to you succeeding than I am to not hurting your feelings." This does not mean that I go out of my way to hurt your feelings ... it does mean that so often it's our feelings (low self-esteem, negative beliefs about being wealthy, deserving etc.) that have got us into the crap we might find ourselves in in the first place. So yeah, there are times when I shove them under your nose and ask "Do you still want to do this shit or are you ready to move on?!"

So we challenge people, in a supportive and constructive way, to take themselves on in an environment and business model that WANTS them to get to the top. In a traditional business model, if you told your boss you were going to take their job, I wonder how comfortable they would be with that idea!

So what's possible?

To begin with, I have to prequalify this by saying that different companies have different payment plans, so it's impossible to give a "one size fits all" response. However, on a programme called Mind Your Own Business©, the intention of it is that after 90 days, the individual will have a solid platform from which they will either be able to leave their job or most definitely have a clear path to when they will be able to leave their job.

The sole focus of the course is to create core competencies and the approach is the same as though this was a second job ... i.e. that each individual gets to work and applies themselves <u>fully</u> to each of these competencies until they become competent, <u>not</u> "it's my business so I will do it in my own sweet time" ... this is imperative because it's the action people take (or don't take) that is going to determine their outcome. It should go without saying, but whichever option you take after reading this book, you <u>have GOT to realise that you need new skill sets to create a new outcome</u>.

What impact would it have on your life if after 90 days you either quit your job or had clear sight as to <u>when</u> you could quit?

Imagine if you are in a position where your salary is matched by the income you generate in your business and you still go to work because you truly love it! The freedom it gives you is remarkable, because it then takes away any dependency on needing to work for money.

Whichever choice you make, the point is that the intention is for our students to reach the end of the 90 days and to have the <u>choice</u> as to whether they want to quit their job and step off the hamster wheel ... for the rest of their lives.

90 days. Look at your diary and genuinely notice what date that would be, from right now.

THIS IS WHERE YOU GET YOUR LIFE BACK.

As a father of five, the one area where this made the biggest single difference was the beginning of the day. To be able to give my children the attention and the time to get them off to school, without me needing to bust a gut to get off to some meeting or other, was a real joy. When you add to this the constant feeling of security, knowing that your outgoings are covered even before the month has started, then you begin to realise that it is the peace, the time and the security that underpin your life ... and that each month you can go on and play

the game of creating more options, more
possibilities.

However, to get to that position you have to work,
you have to plan, you have to set time aside and
dedicate yourself to learning. Here's an absolute
truth: If you are not prepared to put everything into
90 days (part-time too!) for the chance of creating
that outcome, then give this book to someone
else.

For further information, go to Author's
Recommendations and check out The Mellow
Marketing Company and the Integrated Marketing
System©

"Individual commitment to a group effort, that is what makes a team work, a company work, a society work, a civilisation work."

Vince Lombardi

Chapter 11

What Are You Here For?

What a ride eh?!

We've travelled a long way and covered a huge amount of information. I'm sure you can now see why I needed to write this. In fact, I hope you feel compelled to bring this information to the attention of others, so that they too can make up their own minds. We need to collectively avert a huge amount of possible suffering, stress and social unrest that will happen unless we are proactive.

However, before we "wrap it up", I want to ask you something that will surprise you ...

What if there were no tsunami?

What if all these people are wrong?

I don't believe Mark Carney or Barack Obama would have said these things if they did not believe them to be the case, but ... if all these people were wrong, and jobs were maintained, even new ones created ... now that you can see what it's like to surf, would you stay in Job 1.0?

Just imagine this scenario:

You check into your online bank account and discover that while you have been reading this book, your monthly salary has been doubled by people you have never met having purchased from your business.

Now imagine that happening three or four times a month.

Now imagine that happening twice a week, every week, and notice how you feel. Notice the stress leaving your body as you realise that you don't have to work to someone else's plan or worry about whether you can pay the rent or the mortgage.

Now imagine paying off the mortgage. And having serious levels of savings.

Or how about taking next week off and going somewhere you have always wanted to go ... with friends, family or loved ones ... just because you can.

Then there are the little things ... like having a start to the day that is not prompted by you needing to get up at a fixed time but instead at your own leisure. What impact would that have on you? If you have children, what difference would that make to their day too?

That's what it's like. It's not just about the money; it's about choice, about getting your life back. You will certainly have worked for it, but from the outset you were clear in your mind and your heart that it was going to be worth it.

If you are struggling with this notion, then let me assure you, it's not because this is unrealistic, it's because your imagination has been too restricted for too long.

"'You can't depend on your eyes when your imagination is out of focus."

Mark Twain

What matters to you about your life? What do you want your life to be about? Getting by? Managing? Coping? Or finding out who you are, what you are capable of and living in a world of stepping up and out, where the prize is that you get to look and SEE yourself in the mirror looking back, knowing that the satisfaction of making it happen is completely liberating?

So many people are living lives of quiet desperation: "tiptoeing through life, hoping to make it safely to death" was a phrase I heard that hurt, but said it like it is for so many. The truth is that those people are dead already, lost in their own flea circus with the lid firmly screwed on and the air running out.

In my coaching work, the first thing that I say to a client (the company) is to expect people to leave because, to me, there is nothing worse than seeing someone with a compromised soul. If nothing else in life, the thing I am compelled to do is to take the lids off and smash people's jars.

My initial background was as a trained classical musician. I played the cello and piano from the age of six. I was good but I wasn't brilliant and it was down to me having some talent but more so being a good student ... actually, scrap that, an <u>obedient</u> student as I practiced both instruments every day without being asked.

Everyone, including me, assumed that my musical future was carved out before me, so it was "interesting" that on the very day that I was offered a place at university to read music, I quit. Completely.

It took me decades to realise that the reason I had stuck at it so dutifully was because I got approval by doing so and in a family where I was very much the "troublesome twin", approval was in desperately short supply. I make this point to illustrate that sometimes we do things for unconscious reasons, which are at odds with what our natural talents are capable of delivering for us. (If you know you are not achieving the level of reward that your talents should be creating, it's because you have an unconscious need running.)

Once I had realised that my motivation was messed up, I not only quit without any regret, but the message I got from it became (and still is) the main driver in my coaching ... the message was ...

"'We've all got our own tune inside of us and yet we go around playing other people's music.''

Now, with all these options in front of you, you can dream, plan and action a way of life that will leave you in daily appreciation because you are living and creating. Integrated Marketing removes all excuses. Without excuses, there is nowhere to hide ... and why would you want to anyway?

Are you going to make mistakes? 100% yes. So what? We all have, do and will continue to do so. But this time, by getting clear about what matters and creating a game to play, you win some or you learn some, so you cannot lose.

In addition, with most of these options you can explore them initially for free, either by attending a free one-day seminar, downloading further free information or joining a free webinar. So start with that, right now.

If you are someone who has been frustrated and wants more out of life, this is for you. If you are a woman and a mother, then this is for you. If you are a father and want more time with your family, then this is for you. If you are a single parent and you want security and independence for you and your family, then this is for you.

If you have insufficient pension funds, whether you are retired already or are planning ahead, then this is for you.

In addition, another real benefit of Integrated Marketing is that it involves people. I am a classic case of where this is of benefit. Being divorced and my children having grown up and left home, I find myself in a situation where having people around me who are all collectively involved with something that has a purpose offers me an opportunity to engage with a new phase of my life. I also would suggest that new parents look at this because one of the biggest shocks of being a new parent is the sudden falling away of your work and social situation.

If you are a student about to go to college ... before you go, then this is for you. (The amount of college students who drop out because their online business is making them way more than their lecturers is hilarious!) The "normal" route is to take a year out and then go to college. Now, take a year to build your online business and see if you still want to go to college.

If you have never succeeded at school then this is for you.

And if you are reading this and you have a feeling ... literally, a feeeeeeling inside of you that you know you deserve something more, something better, not just financially but that you want to look yourself in the mirror and see the person you KNOW yourself to be ... then this is for you.

In my own business, I make a point of calling people out. We are in a fight at the moment folks and there is a real sense of urgency to let people know that there is a new future, right now. If they aren't aware of this, then you now know that they will most likely get washed away. This is why I believe that we have a collective responsibility. Finally, we are in a time where "we the people" really does mean that we the people can make a difference, without needing to resort to any other body, or group.

On a final note, as I set out to write this book, I always thought that I would conclude it with a final flourish, tying it all together with a nifty one-liner phrase and exit with a majorly cool, "Obama out" style mic drop.

Instead, what I recognised along the way was that there is a deeper and more poignant message even than that there is a tsunami coming. After centuries of conditioning, we are finally at a point where our personal liberation is there for the taking, along with the responsibility to fully engage with and take ownership of this incredible Life we have been given in a time of unparalleled opportunity.

The absolute fact is that we no longer have to live a life of restriction, like the flea conditioned in a jar with the lid screwed on, and that with the technology now accessible to billions of people, each one of us has an equal playing field, free from prejudice of any kind.

In truth, there is a way bigger message that the fear of the oncoming devastation is causing many people to focus their minds on and finally realise (it's bizarre how we often need fear to focus our minds). But before I leave you with it, I want to sincerely wish for you, with every fibre of my being, that whatever your choice, your onward journey in Life is a liberating and enriching one.

So with that ... the simple truth is ...

You are free to choose a new way of life and ...

There is no jar.

"The most important kind of freedom is to be what you really are. You trade in your reality for a role. You trade in your sense for an act. You give up your ability to feel, and in exchange, put on a mask. There can't be any large-scale revolution until there's a personal revolution, on an individual level. It's got to happen inside first."

Jim Morrison

About The Author

Many people talk about manifestation but few play the game in the way that Paul Hornsey-Pennell does...

At the age of 7, he had a thought: "One day, I will live up a farm track, in a farm cottage, in Hampshire and I will write a book." All of this happened in 1994 and the book was an international bestseller.

Recognising that this was more than "a coincidence", he deciphered the process that enables manifesting to a seemingly miraculous degree and he applied them to himself, focusing on having a rich and varied life.

As he became a bestselling author, presenter, public speaker and multiple business owner, as well as a father of five children, it could be said that he succeeded.

But it was after "just talking to" an addict for less than an hour, resulting in them quitting heroine for good, that his passion for connective coaching was ignited. For 25 years, his surreal and intuitive style - not for the faint-hearted - has focused on the elite in international sport, music and business, but his passion has always been for "the little guy" (men and women) setting out on their own.

Applauding the courage it takes for an individual to step up and decide to make their mark in the world of business, Paul constantly searched for systems, processes and models to stack the odds more in their favour, along with running his "Dare To Dream" mindset courses.

Now, "Surfing The Techno-Tsunami" firmly places Paul Hornsey-Pennell in the category of "thought leader" and makes its own clear statement of a new path forward, combining technology with mindset, holding the hand of the reader as they are exposed to a new, challenging and exciting world.

Even as a boy, he regarded "the job" as demanding too much time for too little in return, imposing loyalty, crushing spontaneity and taking people away from their families. So he searched for a model that works for the individual AND the company, but there was one problem that needed to be addressed.

Having coached thousands of people over the years, his experience told him that 80% of people do not identify themselves as, nor in fact want to be, an entrepreneur.

Recognising the devastation that many anticipate the techno-tsunami is going to have on jobs around the world, he knew that it was not acceptable to leave the 80% behind. So as he became involved with some of the giants in internet marketing, he developed simple, effective solutions that are uniquely for both the entrepreneur and the "non-entrepreneur".

The thinking behind this is both logical and clever. If you are someone who does not identify as an entrepreneur, you are going to relate to the solutions in this book ... and if you are an entrepreneur, you want/need to know the solutions that will appeal to "non-entrepreneurs" as they begin to urgently search in their millions in the face of increasing mass redundancy.

So, with the tsunami fast approaching, it looks like it's not the only thing that's just about to create some waves.

"Everything Great That Happened In This World
First Happened In Someone's Imagination."

Astrid Lindgren

Author's Recommendations

All the following entries are from some of the Individuals and companies that have been commented upon within the book.

Whilst it is impossible to promise results, as this is mostly down to each individual's attitude, focus and intention, it is possible to not only affirm that their courses are of the highest calibre in their respective fields but also, from the author's perspective, to affirm that each one of these individuals gives 100% in their commitment to enable others to step into the remarkable possibilities that they offer.

Check each out, ask questions and, where a free/low-cost day or event is offered, then go, research and arrive at your own decision from being informed.

Wishing you good fortune and a wonderful journey,

Paul

Welcome to the Home of Integrated Marketing

IMAGINE... in <u>ONLY 90 DAYS</u> from NOW...

You have the bedrock of your online business...

with SOLID CONSISTENT momentum and growth from ONLY (incredibly) 30 customers

AND a support team <u>adding more</u> to your business.

You are ALREADY in a position to either <u>LEAVE YOUR JOB</u> or know <u>precisely</u> when you can... (if you want to!)

Our unique MindYourOwnBusiness© programme and Integrated Marketing System© are for both the "newbie/non-entrepreneur" AND the experienced entrepreneur looking for a powerful model to work with.

We were NEVER meant to work so hard, for so long, for so little...

Get Your LIFE back!

Make it YOUR business to find out about OUR business...

<u>www.themellowmarketingcompany.com</u>

"... because Life isn't meant to be stressful"

The 7 Elements Of Wealth

Embark On a Journey To Health, Wealth, Relationships, Fulfilment & Happiness

With **Ed J C Smith**, Multi 7-figure Business Owner

Today most people dream of earning more money, having more freedom and doing more of what they want to do and less of what they don't want to do.

However, most people struggle to ever make this an actual reality.

This training will give you everything you need to achieve and master in the most important areas in your life, so you can really live a life that is fulfilled and complete.

JOIN NOW FOR TODAY'S SPECIAL OFFER
at **www.bit.ly/php7EoW**

You will receive:

- Access to the private online training program with over 49 modules.
- Step-by-step training to help you master the 7 Elements of Health, Wealth, Relationships, Fulfilment and Happiness.
- A walkthrough that enables you to truly start to see massive differences in your life and your ability to create results.
- An approach to gain financial freedom as well as emotional freedom.

Total Package Value: £1,497   Today's Special Offer: **£49**

30 Day Money Back guarantee

I know you are going to love it and I am that confident that you are going to be blown away. If for whatever reason you are not blown away with the program you can get all of your money back.

PROPERTY INVESTING FAST TRACK

FREE One-Day Property Training Course

With **Paul Preston**,

One of the UK's Leading Property Experts

Here's what you'll discover on the day:

- How to get started in property without needing a lot of money
- How YOU TOO can make BIG MONEY from property
- Finding Big Discount property deals in your area
- The HIGH cash flow models for BIG profits
- How to build a real business - one that works for you
- The tools, techniques and system you need for success.

The One-Day 'Property Investing Fast Track' will give you both the tools, AND the confidence you need to get started in property.

And remember...you DON'T need a lot of money to get started...!

Paul Preston
Property Expert & Mentor
Guinness World Record Holder
Property Coach of the Year
UK Speaker of the Year

Grab Your **FREE** Tickets now at:
www.PropertyTrainingCourse.co.uk

And join the Property Success Community Group on Facebook
www.bit.ly/ppinvitation

15378885R00109

Printed in Great Britain
by Amazon